C
P
TEXTURES
TECHNIQUES
FOR SURFACE
DESIGN

Laurence King Publishing

LAURENCE KING

Published in 2017 by
Laurence King Publishing Ltd
361–373 City Road
London EC1V 1LR
e-mail: enquiries@laurenceking.com
www.laurenceking.com

This book was designed and produced by
Laurence King Publishing Ltd, London.

A catalogue record for this book is available from the
British Library.

ISBN: 978-1-78067-861-0

Design: Alexandre Coco
Picture research: Nick Wheldon and the author

Principal photography by Meidad Suchovolski

Printed in China

Contents

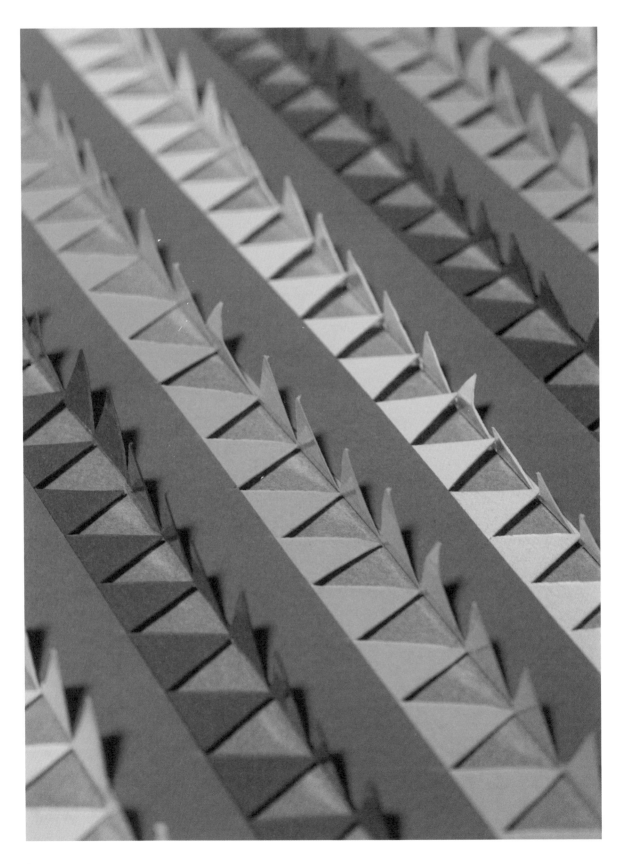

Introduction

Materials such as wood, clay, metal, fabric and plastic are frequently used to create textured surfaces that are crumpled, woven, flecked, frayed, pleated, corrugated, rippled, ribbed, slit, scored and more, either for decorative effect or for a functional purpose.

Paper, however, is rarely used to create a textured surface. Perhaps this is because it is often considered fragile, ephemeral or downright ordinary when compared to materials with more intrinsic textural beauty and longevity. Or perhaps we are too quick to accept paper's traditional roles as a ground (for printing and drawing on) or as a structural material (for making origami, pop-ups, packaging and the like) to look for other uses.

And yet, its unmatched chameleonlike ability to be transformed by folding and/or cutting gives paper a great advantage over other materials. Of all materials, I suggest that paper is the least used but the best suited for creating surface textures. It has no serious rival. Once created, paper textures can be used as the inspiration for two-dimensional prints and bas-relief surfaces in other materials, with many art and design applications.

The book is intended to have a broad appeal, from professional designers and makers to students of design and even school students of any age, as well as providing material for their teachers. Unlike origami and pop-ups, almost all the techniques presented require little or no technical knowledge or precision and they can be made by both the most experienced and the youngest of hands. Further, the techniques are very creative, quick to make, inexpensive and, well, fun!

The structure of the book closely follows projects I have run in colleges of design for more than 30 years. Each of the 12 chapters shows how to make a different surface texture, evolving from basic white-only examples through two-colour to multicolour samples, concluding with examples from artists and designers. The final selection was chosen to offer the greatest diversity of possibilities – flat, relief, geometric, organic, simple and complex. These examples are not necessarily finished in, or made of, paper, but the techniques are the same and the pieces may well have been modelled in paper first.

It is my hope that this book will open for its readers the infinite possibilities of using paper as a textural material, leading in turn to the creation of many innovative and successful works of art and design.

Paul Jackson

The Twelve Paper Texture Techniques … and More

This book shows how paper can be used to create textured surfaces using 12 different techniques. Each technique has its own chapter. Each chapter shows first the technique, then demonstrates how that technique can be used to create A6-sized (15 x 10.5cm/6 x 4in) white samples with 80gsm copy paper, how to make larger-sized coloured samples from a variety of papers, then, finally, how those samples can be used as inspiration to create works of art and design in paper or other materials.

These 12 techniques are not a complete list, but represent a broad cross-section of diverse texturing possibilities. With a little thought, a further 12 could be created, then 12 more, and so on. Here are some ideas for further textures:

Embossing – 3D weaving – Printed surfaces – Braiding – Shredding – Folding curves – Boxes – Cones – Origami forms as a repeat texture – Tubes, rings or circles – Wet or chewed paper – Hole punching – Pop-ups – Origami tessellations or corrugations

In addition to the white and coloured samples presented in the book, try these ideas:

Mix together different white papers – Mix together two different textures – Use paint, pastel or crayon to create coloured surfaces – Mix different media, such as paper, foil, nylon and fabric – Change the scale, perhaps scaling-up an A6 sample to A1 – Make a cast of a surface using papier mâché, latex, plasticine, clay or another material – Don't use paper at all!

Ideas for Developing Samples into Pieces of Work

You probably have an idea already of what you want to make – an artwork, or perhaps apparel, furniture, jewellery, a print or a ceramic tile. However, if you want to create paper textures for the pure pleasure of making them, here are some ideas to lead you towards your final pieces of work.

Make a photographic record of the textures. Photographs of paper textures are often as aesthetic as the textures themselves and make an excellent addition to project notebooks or worksheets.

Scan or photocopy the textures. Experiment with a scanner or photocopier to create images that can be digitally manipulated to create final prints. One advantage of working digitally is that small details of texture almost unnoticeable to the eye can be greatly enlarged to extraordinary effect. These prints can be copied on to fabric.

Draw the textures. Drawing is an excellent way to look properly at what has been made and, by doing so, to perceive the next step in developing final work. Drawing is not an end in itself, but a way to understand your work better.

Develop textures for use as backgrounds. Consider developing paper textures against which to photograph accessories such as bags, scarves or jewellery. Textures can also be used as backgrounds for web pages, posters and other two-dimensional graphic surfaces, or developed as textured typefaces.

Use another material. Make a series of experiments with other materials to see how textures made first with paper can be remade in fabric, cardboard, polypropylene, wood, ceramic and more. Techniques can rarely be directly copied from one material to another, so reinterpreting the technique requires as much creativity – probably more – than making the original surface in paper.

Notes for Teachers

Although this book has been written primarily for students of art and design and practising artists and designers, making textures from paper can be taught from the early years of school to higher education courses for students of art and design.

A paper-textures project can be set up with a minimum of expense, resources and time, and, at the end of a session, waste is minimal and easily cleared, thus maximizing the working time. Creating textures requires only basic hand skills, so makes an ideal project for students of any age unused to hand-intensive making activities.

There are many formats for a paper-textures project, adaptable to the available time and resources, and the age of the students. Here are a few ideas, which should also be useful for readers who are working individually with the book and who are looking for ways to further extend the ideas presented on its pages.

Let the students name the textures they make.
Do not give students a list of names for textures such as 'stippling' or 'tearing', but let them think of names for themselves. Usually, the simpler and more concise the name, the clearer the task becomes, with different textures appearing more distinct.

One technique per student. Instead of giving each student 12 or more textures to make – which would create a very lengthy project – each student is given only one texture to make. That texture can then be developed through as many different samples, scales and materials as required.

Display ideas. Panels of paper textures – particularly the white textures – look beautiful when displayed in large groups, especially when lit carefully. The groups can be the same texture or a mix of different ones.

An antidote to digital media. A paper-textures project enables participants to understand how paper folds, bends, tears, cuts and feels to the touch, better, perhaps, than any other activity. The educational benefits of this hands-on experience should not be underestimated in today's digital design environment. Let's not forget that 'digital' comes from the Latin *digitus* (finger). Thus 'digital design' is literally 'finger design' – which is what this book is all about.

1

Twisting

Narrow strips of paper can either be rubbed tightly between the fingers to create dense lengths of paper string, or twisted around and around more roughly to create a more textured surface. These lengths may then be glued individually to a backing sheet. They may also be plaited, twisted, woven or knitted together to create paper rope, or paper fabric, which will have surprising strength and durability.

The conversion of a sheet of paper into a linear form and then back to a two-dimensional surface is a particularly pleasing series of transformations.

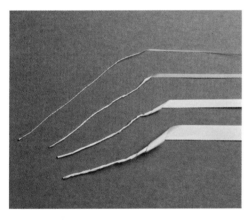

Paper can be shredded into strips of different thicknesses, then twisted back and forth between finger and thumb to create lengths with different textures. With care, widths as narrow as 2mm ($^{1}/_{16}$in) may be cut.

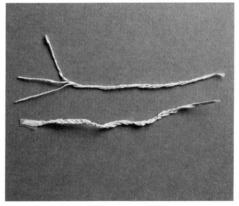

Three separately twisted strands may be plaited together to create a thicker strand, which in turn may be plaited together, and so on. These strands, although made from fragile strips, have remarkable strength.

1.1
White Textures

When twisted, or twisted together, strands of white paper make a wide variety of expressive textured surfaces. The essential contradiction of a line making a plane of texture gives great scope for experimentation and surprise. This is one of those techniques in which a lack of fine motor control may actually be an advantage, as it permits the creation of exaggeratedly animated surfaces.

1.1_1
Loosely twisted lengths of previously twisted paper, of different thicknesses, are coiled into spirals of varying sizes. The careful packing of the spirals creates a dense surface, somewhere between a texture and a pattern.

1.1_2
Lengths of paper are twisted in several different ways – tightly, loosely, neatly, roughly – to create a texture that is clearly linear, but does not repeat from element to element.

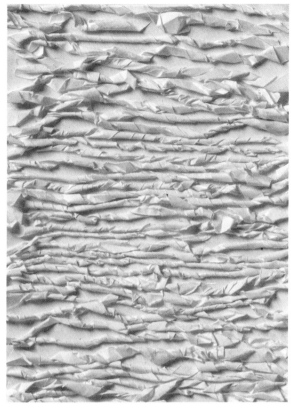

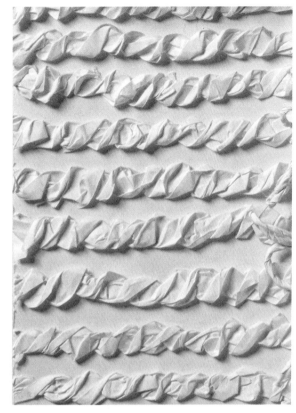

1.1_3 (above left)
Thin strands of different widths were cut and
twisted almost identically, then laid out in
neat horizontal bands. Note how the strands
are not packed tightly together, but laid
loosely side by side.

1.1_4 (above right)
Instead of twisting a length of paper to create
a cylinder, the paper was first twisted and
then flattened in a manner that was almost
folded, then twisted again, producing an
unusual texture.

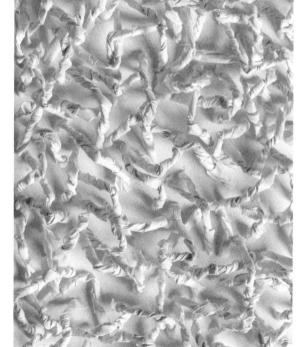

1.1_5
Narrow lengths of twisted paper are allowed
to loop up (towards the camera), then down
to the backing surface to create a three-
dimensional texture with a lot of space
under and between the threads.

1.2
Two-colour Textures

With the possibility of creating contrasts between colours comes the possibility of creating surfaces from twisted threads that are very yarnlike in appearance, almost knitted or woven. Consequently, the paper surfaces often appear to be soft to the touch (though they are not!).

1.2_1
Near-identical spirals of twisted paper are laid out next to each other to create a tight surface. The occasional use of off-white spirals among the more numerous darker ones gives visual interest to an otherwise monochrome surface.

1.2_2
Alternating bands of light and dark twisted threads are simply arranged in a configuration that suggests tree bark, or perhaps a fingerprint, but which is still more of a field of texture than a repeat pattern.

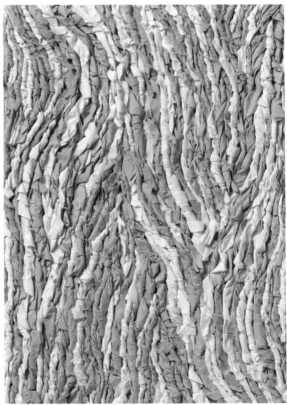

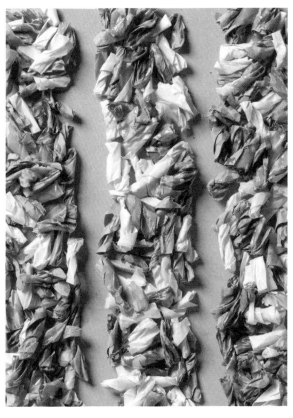

1.2_3 (above)
Short lengths of roughly made twists are arranged in neat columns, separated by blank areas of the backing sheet that lend calm and order to an otherwise frenetic surface.

1.2_4 (below)
Similar to 1.2_2, this texture is simpler and calmer. The subtle use of twists of different widths adds a sense of receding space to what would otherwise have been a flat, uniform surface.

1.3
Multicolour Textures

The textures shown here are made from a mixture of papers and metal foils (aluminium kitchen foil and copper foil). They are included to encourage you to experiment with materials, to look around and use whatever is to hand, however unlikely it may seem. Often, the use of unlikely materials gives character and quality to what might otherwise be a conventional texture. Be adventurous!

1.3_1
A mix of aluminium foil and beige and off-white papers combine to create this scintillating texture. Note how the different surfaces reflect and absorb light to create areas of activity and rest.

1.3_2
The backing sheet, made from aluminium foil, holds the texture together, filling in the spaces between the sparsely arranged aluminium twists. Note how the paper twists spiral around the aluminium.

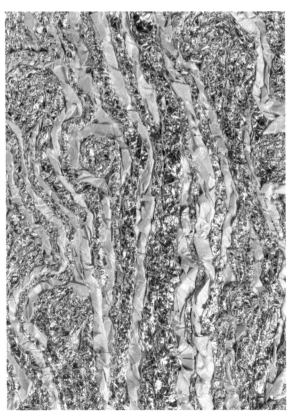

1.3_3
Copper foil, being thicker than aluminium foil,
cannot twist as tightly, so this surface is less
detailed than the previous samples. The effect
is to create a calmer, chunkier texture.

1.3_4
Using the same combination of materials as
1.3_3, this surface sees the copper foil and the
papers cut into shorter sections to create a
less sinewy, more chopped-up surface.

1.4
Taking it Further

Thread, string or rope made from materials such as cotton, nylon line or metal wire have always been made from finer threads twisted together, thus the technique of twisting can be said to be one of the most common throughout all areas of design. Pieces that specifically highlight twisting, however, are less common.

1.4_1
Boycotting the Original Content
Strands of paper cut from a book are twisted, then reassembled back into book form. The piece has approximately 30 'pages' and can open like a book. The title gives a context to the work. Valérie Buess (Switzerland).

1.4_2
Twin lengths of very narrow strands of paper are finely twisted at both ends into spiralled clam shapes (each strand creates one ellipse at each end) and the interior surface of each clam shape is painted gold. Dana Bloom (Israel).

1.4_3
A ribbon of silver is turned into a three-dimensional bracelet by a metalworking process known as 'fold forming', which folds and twists the metal into shape. Dianne King (UK).

2

Weaving

The weaving of narrow pieces of cloth, strips of tree bark, slender leaves or grasses into two-dimensional surfaces and three-dimensional objects has a long history around the world. The weaving of paper surfaces fits perfectly into this tradition.

If you are new to weaving, try parallel strips, laid horizontally and vertically, woven into simple 'one under, one over' patterns, before attempting more intricate patterns. You will soon be creating surface textures of great sophistication. Instead of weaving together two lines of strips placed 90 degrees apart, try weaving together three lines, placed 120 degrees apart. Weaving can be addictive!

Here is the most basic 'one over, one under' weave pattern. The two colours have strips of equal width, but either colour or both could have strips of different widths, for extra visual interest.

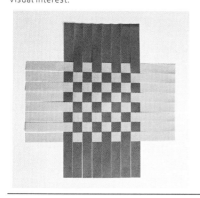

The 'one under, one over' weave pattern can be considerably enlivened by creating strips that are not straight. When woven together, the effect is delightfully eccentric.

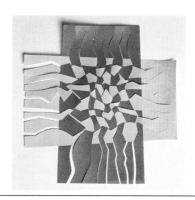

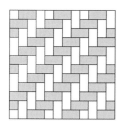

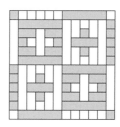
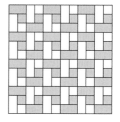

Many other patterns of 'overs' and 'unders' can be created. The activity lies somewhere between puzzle-solving and design, and offers a surprising level of creativity and satisfaction.

2.1
White Textures

Weaving is primarily an activity that creates patterns of colour rather than patterns of light and shade, so weaving white paper only can seem a somewhat contradictory and limited activity. By limiting the colour and tonal palette to white, however, techniques can be explored in a 'pure' way, which will help you make informed choices when colours are introduced.

2.1_1
This playful but precise weave pattern shows how the strips in one direction (in this case, the vertical strips) can be made to dominate the strips in the transverse direction.

2.1_2
Wide vertical strips are woven with narrow horizontal strips. Note how the pattern begins to disintegrate towards the right-hand edge, indicating that the strips needed to have been interwoven with more precision.

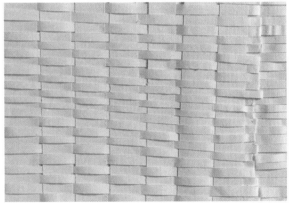

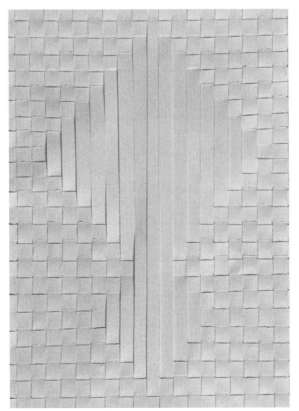

2.1_3 (opposite)
These four images show the possibilities of weaving, from the precise to the ragged, the geometric to free-form. They show, too, how strips can be interwoven in two, three or even more directions. With practice, and a willingness to experiment, weaving paper can be a highly creative and satisfying way to create a surface.

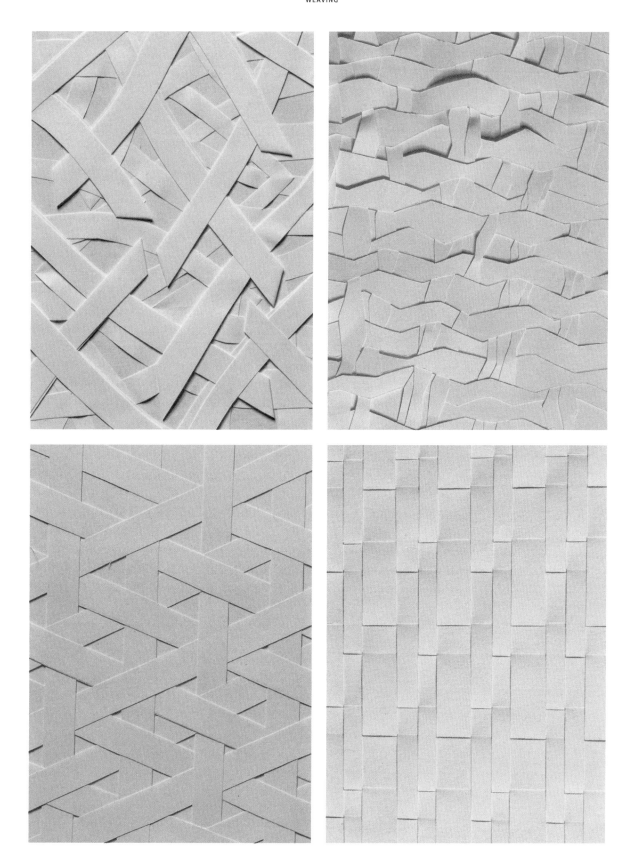

2.2
Two-colour Textures

Unsurprisingly, paper weaving really comes alive when at least two colours are used, permitting the chequerboard effect familiar to anyone who has ever woven in any material. As the examples show, breaking the strict woven grid can be surprisingly simple and effective, so do not hesitate to try something anarchic.

2.2_1
The basic 'under-over' weave is here given form by using papers of contrasting tones and different widths. Note how the darker, wider strips are pressed close together, but the lighter, narrower strips are spaced out, adding to the subtlety of the design.

2.2_2
This weave is a clever mix of random cutting
and structure, making a pictorial surface that
is reminiscent of reflections in a series of
window panes.

2.2_3 (below left)
Strips of different widths are layered together
to create a simple 'under-over' weave. In this
way, the visual effect is achieved not only with
the two colours, but also with the addition of
extra shadows.

2.2_4 (below right)
Instead of using a series of straight strips, the
horizontal pieces are zigzags. When woven
into the vertical strips, this simple device
adds visual complexity to an otherwise
straightforward 'under-over' weave.

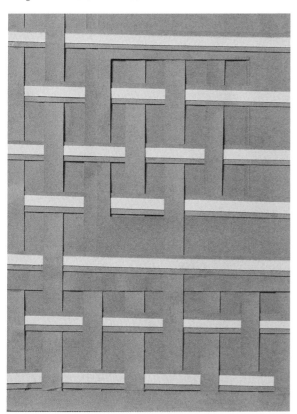

2.3
Multicolour Textures

Two-colour weaves create surfaces that are flat, but multicoloured woven surfaces acquire much more depth. Suddenly, a two-dimensional technique is unexpectedly three-dimensional. The unlimited use of colour also permits the weaving of photographic images, adding many more possibilities to the technique.

2.3_1
The vertical blue strips create a complex surface as they weave through the pink and black strips, laid on a brown background. Note how the horizontal strips are a little imperfectly cut, creating an appealingly handmade look.

2.3_2
This bold, classic weave makes excellent use of only three colours, arranged in a semi-repeat pattern. When weaving, it is tempting to over-complicate the surface, but this sample shows that simple weaves can be successful.

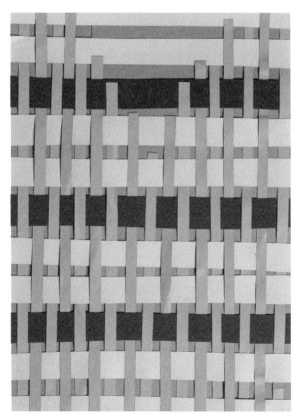

2.3_3 (right)
Dramatic angles add depth and perspective
to these two photographs of buildings,
interwoven together somewhat loosely.
The result is a dizzying surface that is
both architectural and abstract.

2.3_4 (left)
This piece, by the same person as 2.3_3,
is simpler and bolder, resembling more a
collage than a weave. Notice how graphic
elements sometimes continue from one
section to another.

2.4
Taking it Further

Weaving is, arguably, the most common of all manufacturing techniques, so there are abundant examples in everyday life that illustrate how this technique can be applied. Here, though, you can see examples that were chosen because they used not threads, as in cloth, but *widths* of material, more like paper. They differ greatly from each other, showing the variety in the application of this technique.

2.4_1
In his work, the artist weaves together strips of painted paper in mathematical progressions that describe the Fibonacci sequence (1, 1, 2, 3, 5, 8, 13, 21, and so on, the next number in the series being the sum of the two numbers before it) commonly found throughout the natural world. Larry Schulte (USA).

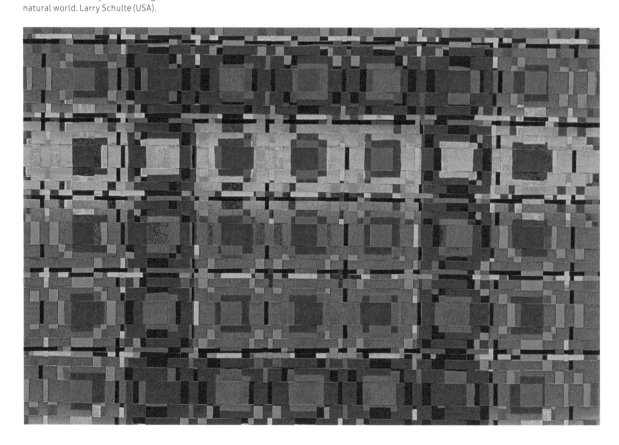

2.4_2
The facade is made from many separate
undulating pieces of aluminium that cleverly
create the illusion of a woven surface. Note
the use of shadows, which add a further
layer of visual interest. Aisaka Architects'
Atelier (Japan).

2.4_3
Woven to resemble basket forms, bulbous
shapes made from steel wrap around the
boiler house that provides power to Guy's
Hospital, London, creating cladding that is
unusually organic. Thomas Heatherwick (UK).

3

Layering

Layering is simply the placing of one piece of paper on top of another. The papers can be glued directly to each other to create a continuous surface, or they can be floated above each other on hidden supports. This latter technique creates larger shadows and thus the layering effect is more easily seen.

The technique comes to life when the layers are not only progressively smaller as the stack rises, but there are also holes in them, creating the illusion of great depth, as though looking into the diminishing perspective of a tunnel. Careful cutting from layer to layer is key to the success of the technique.

The top image shows concentric layers advancing towards the camera and the bottom image shows layers receding.

Using the same concentric technique as on the left, the effect is more dramatic when the layers are separated.

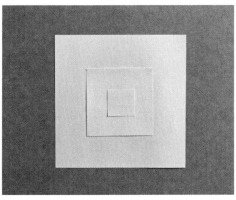

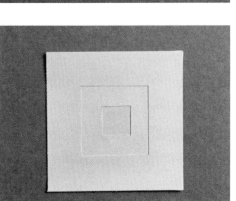

3.1
White
Textures

Layering, of all the paper-texture techniques, requires particularly careful control of the way shadows fall over the surface. The sometimes minimal separation of the layers inevitably focuses attention on the use of light and shade, though the lighting can become less important as the separation increases.

3.1_1
Loosely cut shapes and an informal composition, mixed with a deep separation of the layers, give this piece a playful aesthetic. It can be lit successfully from any angle.

3.1_2
By contrast to the piece on the left, this is cut with great precision and the layers are glued directly together. The careful placement of the light source allows the shadows to be seen.

3.1_3 (above left)
An unconventional layering technique, in which the separate sheets are almost identical in shape and size, though diminishing in size towards the top. Perhaps a better description would be the 'stacking' of paper layers.

3.1_4 (above right)
Precise gluing of hidden supports along the top and bottom edges give this otherwise simple composition great delicacy. Note how the effect would be invisible if the light came from the opposite direction.

3.1_5
The receding perspective effect achieved here is a delicate balance between careful measuring of the cut-out rectangles and an intentionally undulating surface that creates pleasing curves along many of the edges of the paper and, thus, the edges of the shadows.

3.2
Two-colour Textures

The use of a second colour allows the gradation of surfaces to be seen more clearly so that, where applicable, the role of light and shade in defining the edges becomes less important. This opens the possibility for the creation of surfaces that are more like collages than layered contours.

3.2_1 (below left)
The many layers of grey paper are cut freely and descend to the contrasting coloured background, to create a contour effect reminiscent of a geological feature.

3.2_2 (below right)
Here, the pink layers are arranged to protrude over the grey layers, so that the surface is less measured and more spontaneous than the one on the left.

3.2_3 (opposite)
Two colours are used here to create a strong graphic impact. Note how each concentric rectangle is individually designed, including the different separations between the layers.

3.3
Multicolour Textures

As the number of colours increases, the importance of light and shade falling over the layers will decrease, until eventually, colour is everything. Controlling the shape and width of each visible layer is similar to creating different brushstrokes and much expression is possible. What is your preference: to layer geometrically or to layer freely?

3.3_1
A vibrant red contrasts strongly with the other colours to make an unexpectedly flat-looking surface that has great dynamism. The use of pinky-beige relaxes the composition, allowing it to breathe.

3.3_2 (above left)
A simple concentric-rectangle composition is given much added interest by the use of crumpled paper, which both creates a greater separation between the layers (and thus, larger shadows) and softens an otherwise strictly geometric aesthetic.

3.3_3 (above right)
Like its companion to the left, this piece also makes use of crumpled surfaces. Here, the two triangular crumpled areas contrast well with the powerful striped chevron across the middle, creating a surface that is both two- and three-dimensional.

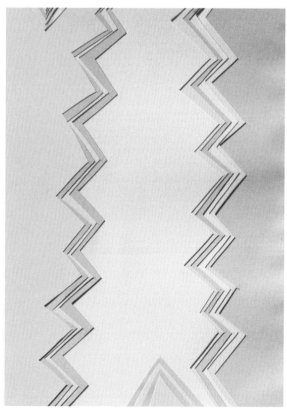

3.3_4
Zigzag edges are glued together in very close formation, separated by flat expanses of colour. Note how the zigzag edges are individually cut (this is not so easy to achieve!) and subtly different.

3.4
Taking it Further

The technique of layering materials offers intriguing possibilities for designers: it uses sheet materials, but instead of the surface being dominant, it is the edges that become so. This reversal of surface and edge creates a language of visual contradiction that can be used to create designs of great originality.

3.4_1
This chair is made from 545 layers of fabric, in almost 100 different colours, individually drawn and then cut with a computer-numerical-controlled (CNC) machine. The shape references rock formations in the Arizona desert. Richard Hutten (Netherlands) for Kvadrat.

3.4_2
Precisely placed layers of slightly separated
sheets of painted aluminium allow the light to
escape from a central cylinder, creating subtle
effects of light and shade. Brian Rasmussen
(Denmark) for Lucente.

3.4_3
Layers of thick black paper interspersed
with hidden sheets of cardboard are lightly
crumpled and folded to create an armchair
described by the designers as 'chaos and
sequence'. Vadim Kibardin (Czech Republic)
for Kibardindesign Studio.

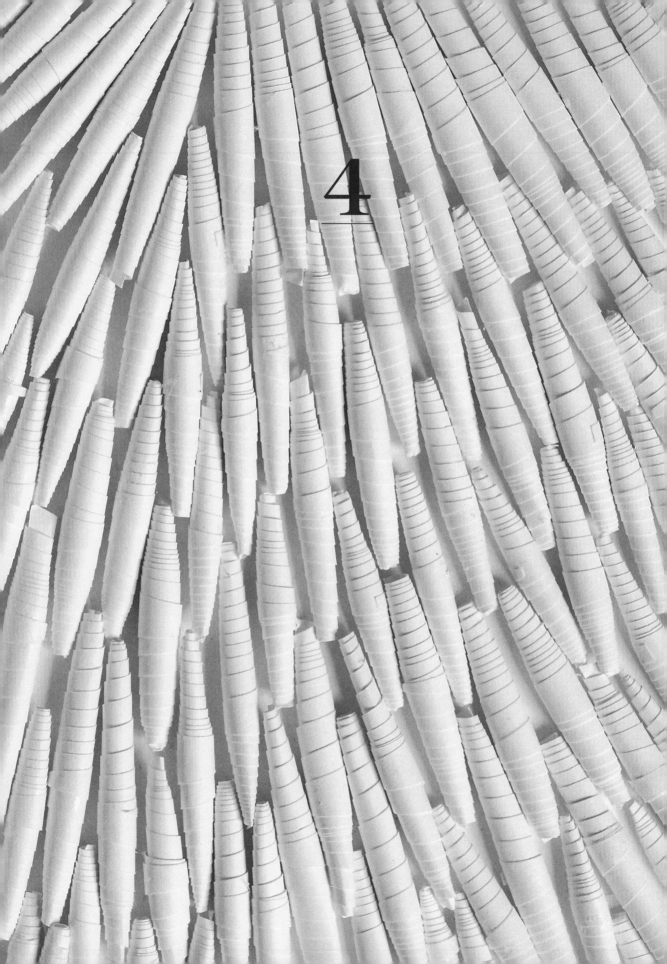

4

Coiling

The technique of rolling long, thin strips of paper into tight or open spirals is sometimes known as 'quilling'. It originated in Europe during the Renaissance as the inexpensive alternative to filigree metalwork. In recent years it has undergone a revival of interest as a decorative art, shedding much of the overly decorative kitschiness with which it had become associated.

There are a surprising number of diverse and creative coiling techniques. Take care not to use excessive amounts of glue when sticking the edge of the paper coil to a backing sheet.

The two groups of quilled spirals here show the two basic techniques of coiling. On the left, the spirals are 'closed' because the end of the spiralling strip is glued down; on the right, the spirals are 'open' and use no glue at all. In all cases, the folds are made by squeezing the spiral between finger and thumb in carefully chosen places.

4.1
White Textures

Coiling is a technique that permits deep shadows to be made across the surface. Thus, even white textures can appear remarkably multitoned and surprisingly dark between, or inside, the spirals. Careful control of the depth of the strip and the tightness of the coil will create these beautiful tonal effects.

4.1_1
These open coils of different sizes and slightly differing depths create a pleasing patchwork of contrasting tones and rhythms, punctuated by the white edges of the rings that are not in shadow.

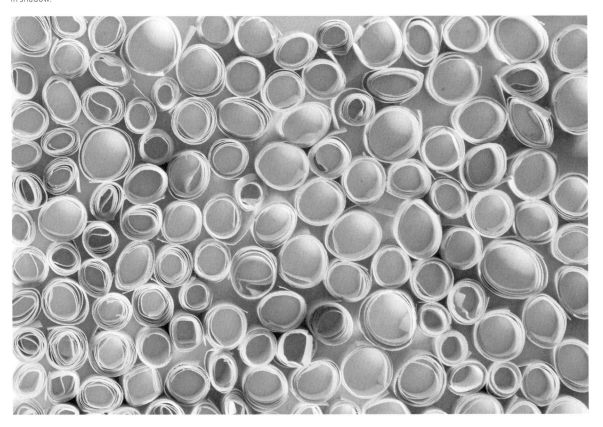

4.1_2
These coils are conical in shape, made by rolling a long, thin triangle of paper. The difference in size and careful composition of the cones gives the texture an extra level of visual interest.

4.1_3 (below left)
One way to create a texture is to lay the coils flat, rather than stand them on end. These coils are made from a very long, very narrow isosceles triangle that allows the paper to bulk up in the middle and narrow at opposite ends.

4.1_4 (below right)
These tall, narrow, tightly coiled, tightly grouped coils create a dramatic cocoonlike texture that is dark and dense. The shadows are unexpectedly dark and will often appear coloured, not grey, depending on the type of 'white' paper used.

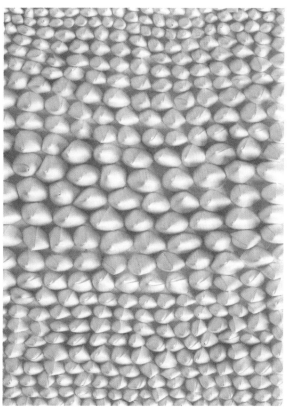

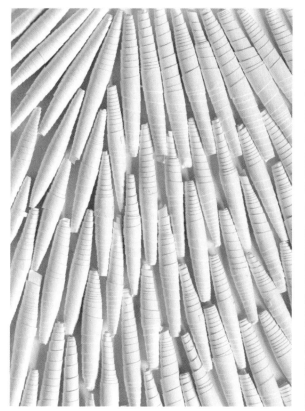

4.2
Two-colour Textures

The linear characteristics of many coiling techniques mean that, unlike many other texturing techniques in the book, it is particularly well suited to making textures that are both decorative and graphic. The introduction of a second colour heightens these characteristics and enables shadows to play an unconventional role as a second level of texture.

4.2_1
The dramatic use of bright red brings alive a quilled texture that would otherwise be difficult to see. Notice how the dark background minimizes the role of shadows in creating the texture.

4.2_2 (above left)
The leaflike motif of open coils bounded by a retaining wall develops into a texture that is elegant and semi-improvised. The similarity of the colours subdues the effect.

4.2_3 (above right)
Long, open S-shaped coils are glued to each other and to the backing sheet to create a carefully organized but still randomly designed texture. The bright backing sheet adds to the graphic impact of the linear coils.

4.2_4
Coils, although abstract, can resemble natural forms when placed in groups. This delicate texture suggests ferns, tendrils or feathers, made more solid by the dark shadows inside the dark coils.

4.3
Multicolour Textures

It is possible to make a much more complex piece than the two-colour works on pages 42 and 43 with the simple addition of only one more colour. With coils, it is all too easy to intend making a sophisticated texture but, by introducing more and more colours, to make that texture ever more decorative and twiddly, until it becomes tawdry. Restraint in the use of colour will ensure a texture remains beautiful.

4.3_1 (below left)
Spirals are connected by uncommonly long lengths of uncoiled paper to create an angled effect that contrasts with the coils. The texture does not fill the rectangular background, which gives it movement and direction.

4.3_2 (below right)
Coils of near-identical shape and size are arranged in a semi-regular pattern and stretched vertically to fill the frame. The precise use of colours gives the pattern form.

4.3_3 (opposite)
A tumbling mass of coils that are tightly wound at the top and become larger and more open as they fall, giving momentum and energy to what would otherwise be a static texture.

4.4
Taking it Further

The technique of coiling when applied to products is surprisingly common, creating an attractive surface that is both functional and decorative. It is, perhaps, less common as a technique for making artworks, but as paper techniques are increasingly appropriated by artists, coiling is becoming more common and accepted. The pieces on these pages represent the best of coiling as a technique for making products and artworks.

4.4_1
Ribbons of beechwood are glued and coiled tightly together around a mould to create a thin skin in the shape of a chair seat and back. The variations in colour in the wood create a natural texture on the surface. Notice how the centre of the coil is left as a small hole, the wood being unable to bend into such tight circles. Anna Štěpánková (Czech Republic).

4.4_2
This dramatic 100kg (220lb), 120cm- (47¼in-) diameter piece is made from coils of folded newspaper packed tightly together. Its imposing scale, mass and weight contradict standard notions of paper as lightweight and delicate, creating a powerful presence. Moshe Gordon (Israel).

5

Tearing

No paper-texturing technique is quite so much fun as tearing. As one of my students once remarked to me, 'Tearing isn't a technique, it's therapy!'

But be careful. Inside this seemingly destructive act is a technique of surprising subtlety, more closely related to drawing than to cutting. The key to controlling how the paper tears is to understand the 'grain' of the paper. Paper is a fibrous mat, in which the fibres line up in parallel. This means that the paper will bend easily along the line of the fibres (because there is little resistance), but will bend less easily *across* the fibres (because there will be more resistance). If you have never noticed this effect before, try it with a variety of papers and cards. The difference can be dramatic.

This difference can also be seen when tearing paper. Paper will tear straight along the line of the fibres, but tears will be uncontrollable and crooked across the fibres (see diagrams below). So, when tearing, the character of the surface you make can be designed. Before you create a textured surface, experiment with tearing the paper in different directions and also, perhaps, at different speeds or by holding the paper close to the tear or far away.

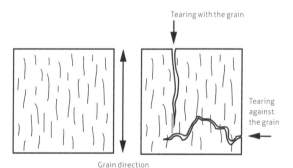

Tearing with the grain

Tearing against the grain

Grain direction

The brown paper (below left) has been torn in three ways to create three different edges. The top edge was torn against a ruler, so that it tore straight and clean. The middle edge was torn against the grain and the bottom edge with the grain. The paper was white, offset-printed with brown ink. Below right is handmade paper with no grain, so the torn edges at the left and bottom are very similar.

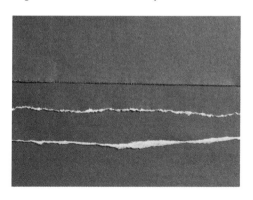

5.1
White
Textures

Tearing paper is not a cut-and-fold technique, but a technique to texture the edges of the sheet. Once torn, the paper can then be used to create almost any texture in this book. The white samples here show how torn edges can be used to create flat, layered surfaces as well as relief surfaces that make a feature of the torn edges. Note how sometimes, the sheet itself is visible, and how, at other times, it can be made almost invisible by the dense packing of edges.

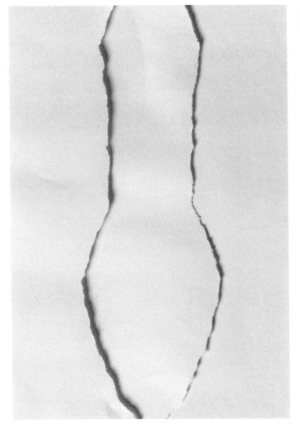

5.1_1
This ingeniously made sample is created by tearing a sheet of paper from top to bottom, then placing one of the pieces on top of the other, but a little to the side, creating a symmetrical pattern. The bottom layer (on the right-hand side of the image) is an added backing sheet.

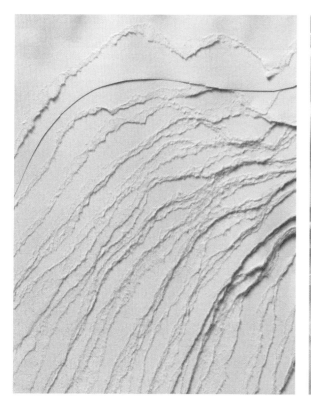

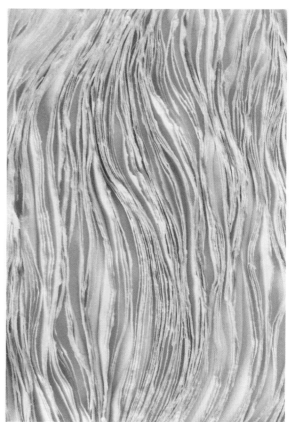

5.1_2 (above left)
Many layers are carefully placed close together to create a surface that is both contoured and sculpted. The use of light and shade is particularly important to show the torn edges to best effect.

5.1_3 (above right)
The fringed effect is created with a great many narrow torn paper strips, glued end-on to a backing sheet. The strips are allowed to pack together randomly or fall open.

5.1_4
Dense, swirling patterns of torn edges are created by gluing narrow strips perpendicular to a base. The gentle curving of the edges and dense packing allows the edges to remain in place with surprising rigidity.

5.2
Two-colour Textures

With two colours, layering one torn edge on top of another of a different colour, alternately, will create many more surfaces and textures than if all the edges are one colour only. The use of two colours is particularly effective when the surfaces are flat, rather than in relief, and when the intervals and shapes between the torn edges are carefully considered, much like the black and white spaces in a Japanese brush painting.

5.2_1
An off-white paper printed with black ink is torn mostly with the grain, but occasionally against the grain , as can be seen twice on the left-hand half of the piece. The tearing is done with great care to expose as much of the off-white paper as possible. Careful positioning of the layers creates a landscapelike effect. Note the use of open areas and the precise placement of just one diagonal tear.

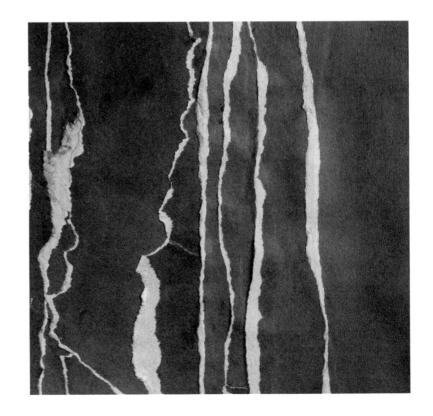

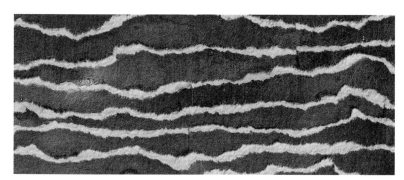

5.2_2 (left)
Green paper coated with black ink is torn and the edges placed horizontally across the piece to create a surface that is both rhythmical and vibrant.

5.2_3 (below)
Uncoated papers are torn both with and against the grain to create an equal balance between the two colours that flattens the surface.

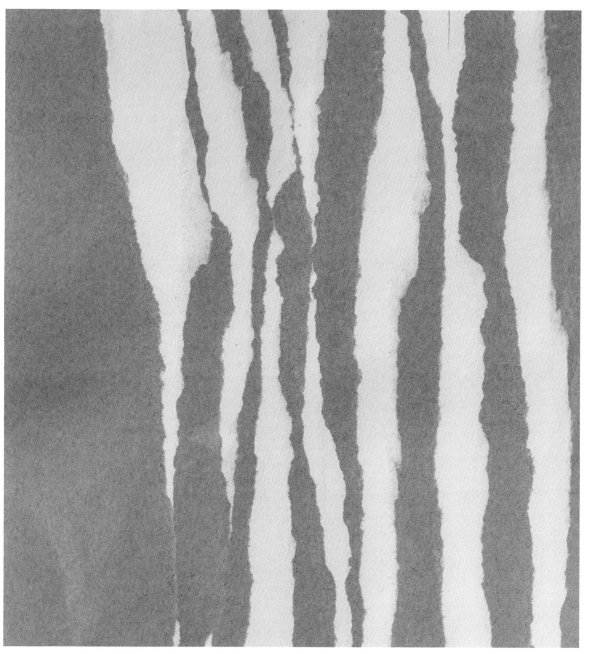

5.3
Multicolour Textures

The use of multicoloured torn edges can give greater depth to the surface texture, so that the plane is not flat but advances and recedes according to the colour. Whereas two colours could only make an alternating pattern, multicoloured surfaces offer a near-infinity of choice. Experiment widely with different papers, coatings and tearing options to discover a sophisticated language of design, far removed from the limitations often associated with tearing.

5.3_1
Three carefully chosen colours create a harmonious composition of large expanses and narrow slivers in which negative and positive spaces interplay well. Look closely and notice how the torn edges are placed with precision. The technique of tearing may itself be a little imprecise but torn edges can still be placed together with sensitivity and accuracy. A designer always has control.

5.3_2 (above)
A collection of bright rainbow colours
carefully torn in a series of diminishing curves
creates a wonderfully vibrant surface, full of
movement and energy.

5.3_3 (right)
Similar to the piece opposite but denser and
with more colours, the torn vertical strip
cleverly divides the surface into two distinct,
but related, halves.

5.4
Taking it Further

A torn edge is simply a textured, irregular edge. Since any surface texture made of paper or any other sheet material must have an edge (or it would stretch into infinity), it follows that torn edges can be used almost anywhere, at any time. They can be used flat, in relief or fully three-dimensional, creating an attractive alternative to a machine aesthetic.

5.4_1 (this page)
The artist takes old shoes and other accessories and covers them with fragments of brightly coloured torn paper. Is the work primarily about giving new life to an unwanted object, or is it mischievously conceptual? There are more questions than answers!
Ida Rak (Israel).

5.4_2 (opposite)
Many layers of hand-dyed silk are stitched together to recreate the texture and sense of movement of a rough-edged brushstroke, combined with an impression of what the layers of a costume might look like if the top encasing layer was cut or torn open.
Felicity Brown (UK).

6

Bending

This is the simplest and quickest of the 12 textures to achieve, but needs to be undertaken with great care so that the bends remain perfect and aesthetically pleasing. More than most techniques, bends rely on good lighting for their effectiveness, so be prepared to experiment with different light sources for maximum effect, allowing shadows to change their position and length.

Done well, bending can be an elegant antidote to the dense patterns of other texturing techniques and should be a number one choice for surfaces that need to be calm and simple.

When paper is made by machine, the fibres lie in parallel. As we discovered with tearing paper (Chapter 5), this creates what is known as the 'grain' of the paper. The grain is crucial to many aspects of paper manipulation, including bending. When the paper is bent *along* the grain, it will bend much more easily than when bent *across* the line of the grain. If you have never seen this phenomenon before, do try it! It's quite a surprise.

Direction of grain

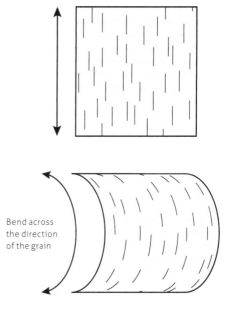

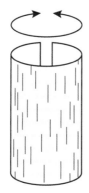

Bend along the direction of the grain

Bend across the direction of the grain

6.1
White Textures

There is a particular purity about a work made by bending white paper. And yet, of all the techniques in the book, this is perhaps the most difficult to achieve: the seeming simplicity of the finished work can only be achieved through control and precision. Understanding the paper's grain is crucial, as is working with light and shade as equal partners.

6.1_1 (left)
Sheets are gently overlaid to create a subtly undulating surface. The effect is enhanced by the use of torn edges to further soften an already delicate surface.

6.1_2 (opposite above left)
Careful gluing of the strips to a backing sheet enables the lengths of bent paper to travel rhythmically across the surface. The positioning of the light at the top left creates shadows both to the side and under the curves.

6.1_3 (opposite above right)
A densely packed surface of twice-bent units creates a texture that is more geometric than others here. The pattern of light and shade would change dramatically if the light source were to move.

6.1_4 (opposite below left)
This improvised composition is not as simple as it may first appear. Note the different ways in which the paper is bent and rolled: sometimes sharply, sometimes barely at all.

6.1_5 (opposite below right)
Is this piece 'bending' narrow strips of paper or should it perhaps be called 'shredding' a sheet? The semi-random arrangement of the strips creates a surface that is both chaotic and structured.

6.2
Two-colour Textures

The introduction of a second colour gives this quiet technique an opportunity to make a little more noise, to be more graphic and to add a wider variety of tones to the shadows. With a wider repertoire of surface possibilities comes the necessity of controlling the bends with greater precision than before.

6.2_1
This unusual corner-view of a bent surface suggests a wafting curtain and has a surprising sense of movement. The second colour is used only minimally, but creates an important silhouette along the bottom edge of the green paper.

6.2_2
Where is the second colour? It is hidden from the head-on camera shot, becoming visible as the background layer when we peep under the curves, and will appear and disappear as we move across the piece.

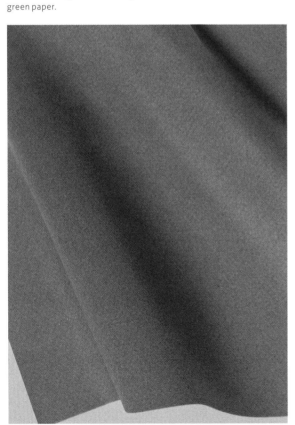

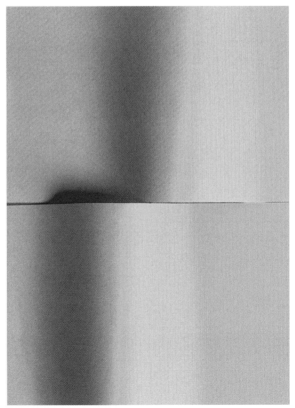

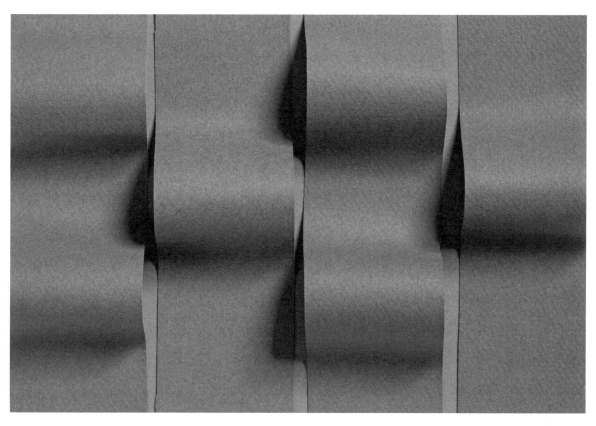

6.2_3
Similar in concept to 6.2_2, this time the bent strips are separated so that the background layer is always visible. The surface thus becomes more playful.

6.2_4
Like 6.2_2, the second colour is invisible from a head-on camera shot, but becomes visible when we move to the left or right and can see under the curves.

6.3
Multicolour Textures

The use of three or more colours means that the technique of bending sheets of paper can now mutate into a technique of bending strips in order to make stripes. Even greater precision when making and gluing the curves is required than when using just one or two colours.

6.3_1
The coloured strips would create a lively surface without being bent, but the addition of the gentle bends – and, in particular, the shadows they create – makes an unusually vibrant texture.

6.3_2
This ultra-simple piece (surely the most minimal sample in the book!) shows three coloured sheets glued together, with just one simple bend down the left edge. Not every texture needs to be frantic. Less is sometimes more.

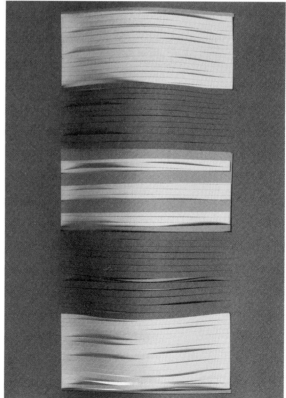

6.3_3
Similar to the piece above, the simple curve is shredded into narrow strips to create, in place of the smooth plane of the original paper, a curve with an unevenness of line.

6.4
Taking it Further

The simplicity and evident purity of the technique mean that its application in design is more difficult than might be anticipated. Somehow, the less there is to work with, the more difficult it is to consider equally the material, the surface texture, the form and the product. However, the examples shown here achieve this admirably.

6.4_1
Made from one sheet of plywood bent into three dimensions with steam, this chair is based on the form of a cowrie shell. It is an extreme example of great simplicity achieved by highly sophisticated means. Brodie Neill (UK) for Made in Ratio.

6.4_2 (right)
A delightful mix of the organized and the chaotic. Many steam-bent strips of varnished oak combine to create a form and texture that are both organic and geometric. Tom Raffield (UK).

6.4_3 (below)
Strips of copy paper are bent and held together with hairpins. As the viewer moves left and right, the dark recesses follow, creating a remarkable flickering effect across the surface. Hadar Rozenbaum, Shenkar College (Israel).

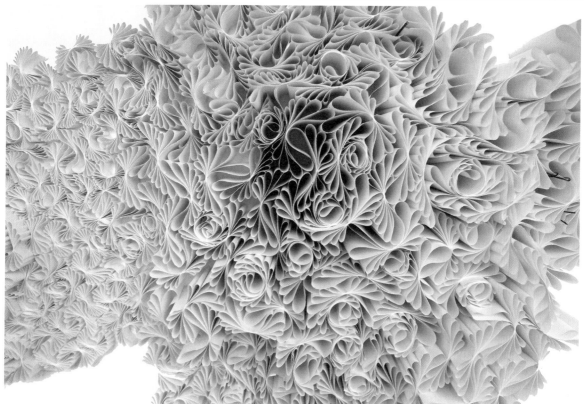

7

Incising and Lifting

This technique relies as much for its effect on good lighting as it does on skilful manipulation of the paper. Shadows are as key for its effectiveness as the paper itself.

The technique has two parts: first, the paper is cut into a non-straight line with a knife (C- or V-shaped cuts are among the simplest); next, either the ends of the cut are joined with a fold that lifts an island of paper bounded by the cut, or the same island is curved delicately upwards. The effect is particularly successful if made as a repeat.

Incised lines must include at least one angle or bend, otherwise there is no loose paper that can be folded or bent backwards. A chevron incision like this will transform into the shapes on the right.

Four examples of how the simple chevron incision can be transformed into free-standing shapes that cast interesting shadows. There are many other ways to manipulate the incision.

An interesting variation is to create an incision that can be lifted in two or more places. The example here has two lifts, but with more complex cuts, the number of lifts can be greatly increased.

These four examples are just some of the ways in which the two lifts can be made. Note the negative–positive effect of the light and shade, as it falls over two opposing lifts.

7.1
White Textures

Incising and lifting is a technique ideally suited for making in white paper, as the lifted shapes react well to light and shade. Even the simplest incisions, when combined together, can create wonderful textural effects. Change the lighting and the texture will change dramatically and, often, unexpectedly.

7.1_1
A simple V incision is here used to great effect on a sheet that is also bent. The combination of the gently lifted Vs and the undulating surface works well.

7.1_2
One long zigzag cut is curled five times to create a series of flickering shadows. The challenge now would be to design further zigzags to the right or left, so that a field of texture could be created.

7.1_3 (above left)
Carefully incised hexagons, with the sixth side left uncut as a fold, are bent delicately upwards. Note how the folds are all parallel, helping to create a tonal uniformity across the surface.

7.1_4 (above right)
Curved incisions that meander back and forth create a delicate rippling effect. A greater density of curves, and lifting them higher, would create a much more graphic use of light and shade.

7.1_5 (right)
Incisions can be made concentrically, then the different sections lifted to different heights. The complex textural effect seen here is further complicated by the absence of a repeat pattern of motifs.

7.2
Two-colour Textures

The potential for incised motifs to create repeat patterns is without limit. Further, when two colours are used instead of one, wonderfully playful textures can be made that rely as much on the interaction between the colours as they do on the effects of light and shade.

7.2_1 (below left)
Careful incising of tiny X-shaped motifs along a predetermined grid, and the careful use of contrasting colours, creates an almost flat, scintillating surface made by minimal means.

7.2_2 (below right)
Concentric incisions create a repeat pattern of goalpostlike motifs, given added interest by changing the background colour from yellow to green down the centre stripe.

7.2_3 (opposite)
This charmingly simple but dramatic texture uses complementary colours to maximize the vibrancy of the surface. Not every successful idea needs to be complex.

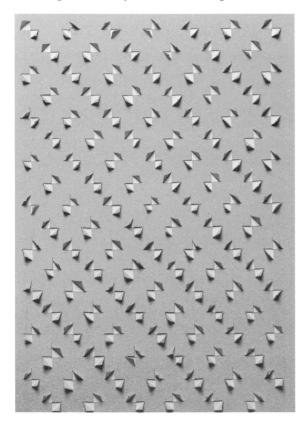

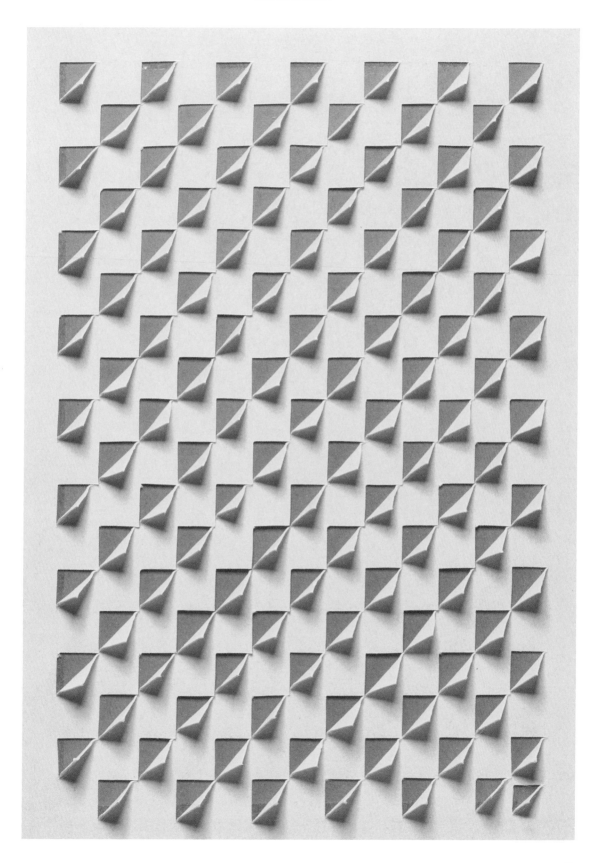

7.3
Multicolour
Textures

The flickering textural effects commonly found in this technique are taken to an extreme when many colours are used. The surfaces become dense, with a kaleidoscope of different colours and many small flaps of paper catching the light and casting shadows. If you like to create detailed surfaces, this technique is for you!

7.3_1 (left)
The first of a suite of three related pieces sees curved tracks of narrow incised Vs separated by arcs of crumpled paper that create a contrasting texture. Light and shade play only a minimal role.

7.3_2 (opposite above left)
In this second piece, straight tracks of V incisions are separated by strips of flower-pattern paper. Unusually for a sample piece, the result is not wholly abstract, but reminiscent of lawns and flowerbeds.

7.3_3 (opposite above right)
This final piece in the suite of three sees the curved tracks of incised Vs ending at the left side with curled flourishes. Experimenting widely with a theme, as here, is the best way to develop final work that is assured.

7.3_4 (opposite below)
A development of the simpler piece on page 73, this variation adds a third colour. The placement of the light source eliminates many of the shadows on the right-hand half of the piece.

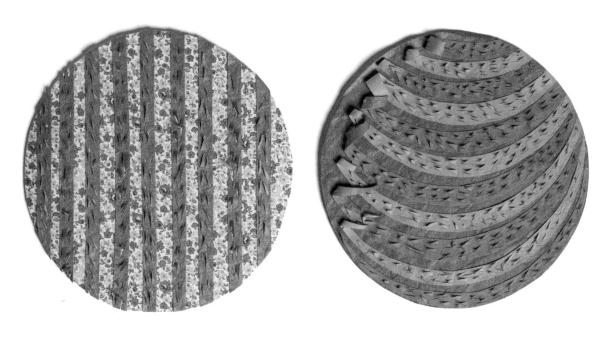

7.4
Taking it Further

More than most texturing techniques, incising and lifting is delicate and wholly reliant on light and shade for its beauty. This makes its application highly detailed and apparently fragile, but, most importantly, a true partner to its light source. Understanding the relationship between the two is the key to using the technique successfully.

7.4_1 (below left and right)
Playful motifs of butterflies and ellipses incised into acrylic and paper respectively, catch the light in different ways when lit externally or internally, bringing the surfaces to life with subtle gradations of tone.
John Lewis Partnership (UK).

7.4_2
This piece achieves its serene effect by the absolute precision of the technique and the strong, oblique lighting, which creates graphic highlights and shadows. The piece is 70 x 70cm (27⅝ x 27⅝in) and made in paper. Geoffrey Nees (Australia).

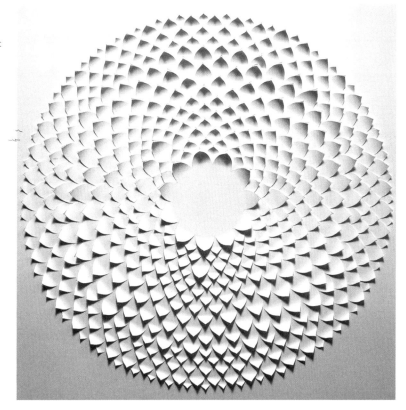

7.4_3
Subtly folded aluminium panels create the illusion of an incised and lifted surface on an open space, several stories high. The external surface of the building in Messe, Basel, is clad in the same way. Herzog & de Meuron (Switzerland).

8

Crumpling

The degree to which paper can be crumpled depends on the thickness of the sheet and the ability of the paper to retain a crease; 80gsm copy paper will crumple better than thicker 160gsm drawing paper, but also better than thinner 45gsm tissue paper, which will barely retain a crease when crumpled. It is well worth experimenting with a variety of papers until you find the one that works best for you, though for convenience, a high-quality 80gsm copy paper is usually a good choice.

Experiment with the length of time for which the paper is crumpled – anything from a split second to 30 minutes. Strange things happen to paper that is crumpled for an excessively long time (try this in a well-ventilated area, as the paper's fibres tend to become airborne).

This is a sheet of copy paper crumpled for just a few seconds. Different papers will crumple in different ways.

The same sheet crumpled for 30 seconds. Not only is the texture denser, but the sheet is shrinking!

The same sheet, crumpled for 15 seconds. Note how the texture begins to become more dense.

The same sheet crumpled for two minutes. The sheet is surprisingly small and now tissuelike to the touch.

The paper was rolled into a tube and pulled repeatedly through the fingers to create this texture of parallel folds.

A paper tube was twisted tightly in the middle, so that only the centre of the paper was crumpled.

8.1
White
Textures

Of all the possible paper textures, perhaps the most totally *textured* effect comes from crumpling white paper. This seemingly destructive act can create surfaces of sublime beauty that change dramatically in character from paper to paper. These surfaces are also very photogenic, not just under the camera, but when scanned or photocopied (open the lid for the best effect).

8.1_1
This crumpled surface resembles animal hide, the surface of a rock or an aerial photograph of a snowy mountain range. Close up, it is immensely detailed, revealing different textural effects at different viewing distances.

8.1_2
The radial texture here was created by collapsing the paper around a fingertip placed in the centre of the paper, then pulling it through the fingers, somewhat like collapsing an umbrella.

8.1_3
Instead of crumpling one sheet, many smaller
sheets can be crumpled up and placed
together to create a much rougher texture
in which many of the edges are visible.

8.1_4
Long channels were creased through a heavily
crumpled surface to create a secondary level
of texture. The combination of the subtle
crumple and the graphic lines gives added
interest for both textures.

8.1_5
A sheet was crumpled, then squashed
between two hard surfaces, collapsing the
gently undulating crumples into a very flat
surface and refolding the undulations as
sharp folds.

8.1_6
The progressively denser texture of crumples
towards the bottom edge of the sheet contrasts
with the emptiness of the background behind,
creating a greater sense of human action than
if the background were removed.

8.2
Two-colour Textures

The use of two colours opens up an opportunity to add a graphic element to the surface (usually heavily diluted watercolour or ink), thus emphasizing the line of the crumple folds. For this effect, the surface does not need to be heavily crumpled and, as can be seen here, many interesting variations are possible.

8.2_1
A crumpled surface made with white paper was dipped into tea, which stained it light brown. The crumples break open the fibres, allowing more staining along the line of the folds than in the areas between them.

8.2_2
A crumpled surface had its crumpled regions delineated with a black pen. The drawing is intuitive and improvised, allowing for regions of different sizes to be emphasized, as the designer wished.

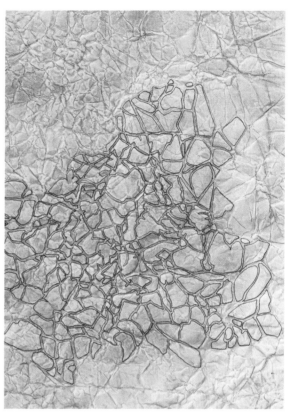

8.2_3 (below left)
Diluted ink was allowed to settle and dry in the crumpled troughs, after which areas of crumpling were painted with more of the same ink. The effect gives the illusion of some depth to the surface, which is actually very shallow.

8.2_4 (below right)
Made in a similar way to the piece on the facing page, but with diluted ink, the surface has also been crushed prior to being inked, thus bringing the folds into sharper relief.

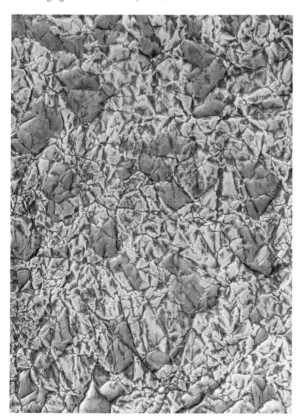

8.3
Multicolour Textures

With the possibility of using an unlimited number of colours, a crumpled surface becomes the ground for a form of textured painting, made with paints, inks and pens. This is the only texture in the book in which the colours are not coloured papers, but colouring agents. Their use is wholly justified, however, by the relation they have with the crumpled surface.

8.3_1
Lines were made with a pen on top of a crumpled surface washed gently in very dilute ink. The blue marks were not made accidentally, but introduced intentionally to add an extra element to the texture.

8.3_2
Looking similar to the image on the left, the lines were not made with a pen. Instead, the whole sheet was washed in diluted ink, after which a solid cream colour was painted into some of the crumpled areas, leaving the 'lines' unpainted.

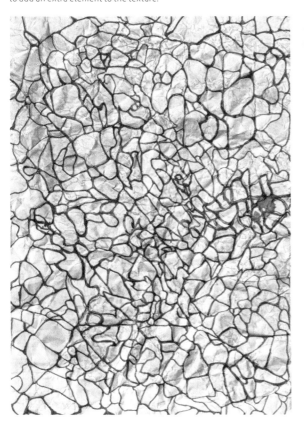

8.3_3
This is a combination of many techniques
seen in this chapter: washes of colour, colour
allowed to sit in troughs, ink run into crumples
– and even flecks of colour added with a brush.
The result is a very sophisticated, sumptuous
surface, made after many experiments.

8.3_4
After washes of diluted inks were brushed
over the crumpled paper, the black lines were
added by rubbing charcoal onto the surface,
then vigorously removing it, so that only the
charcoal impregnated in the lines remained.

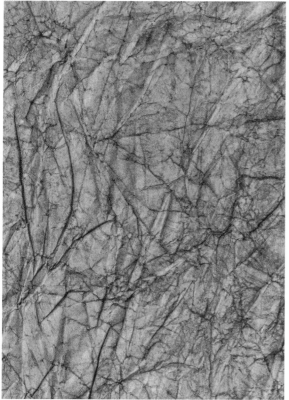

8.4
Taking it Further

Crumpled products almost always look ironic and anarchic, but they are also tactile and vulnerable. They comment on their smooth-surfaced predecessors, but also have a strong character of their own. In recent times, a great many crumpled products have been designed, in many materials, as a welcome alternative to the sleek minimalism of much contemporary design.

8.4_1
The crumples allow the bag to expand to twice its capacity when bulky or heavy objects are paced inside. When removed, the bag snaps back to its original size. The crumples are placed into the fabric by heat and the fabric is biodegradable. kna plus (Japan).

8.4_2
Challenging conventions, this stackable chair wittily declares itself to be the antithesis of good design and sophisticated taste, ironically becoming a design icon itself. The chair is made from compression-moulded wood. Blå Station (Sweden).

8.4_3 (below left and right)
These playful lamps, made in Tyvek®, are sold as crumpled balls, which the purchaser opens and shapes to taste. They can be hung, or placed on a vertical or horizontal surface, remaining heavily crumpled or stretched open. Meirav Barzilay (Israel).

8.4_4 (bottom left and right)
Made from triangles of coloured wood, these rugs can be laid flat as a functional object or crumpled to create an endless number of relief surfaces that can be displayed as works of art. Elisa Strozyk (Germany).

9

Pleating

A simple zigzag pleat – known more formally as an accordion pleat – is easy to make and, with suitable lighting to create strong shadows, will always look dramatic. Accordion pleats can also be created from narrow strips and glued, edge-on, to a backing sheet.

Some pleating patterns are technically very complex, but beautiful textured surfaces can be achieved with a simple accordion – as always, the designer is more important than the technique. To learn many more textural pleat patterns, see the author's book *Complete Pleats: Pleating Techniques for Fashion, Architecture and Design.*

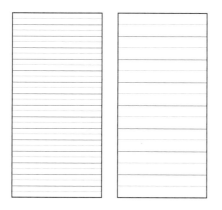

Here are two basic pleat patterns, the red and blue lines representing 'mountain' and 'valley' folds respectively. There can be any number of divisions, but the more there are, the more a surface will appear like a texture and less like a structure.

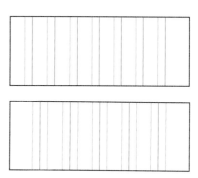

Many other pleat patterns can be made that change the distance between the folds or that change the distribution of mountain and valley folds. They need not always be in parallel – or always be made using rectangular sheets.

9.1
White Textures

White paper, pleat patterns and the careful use of light are natural partners. Few paper-texture techniques offer such a near-certainty that something aesthetic will be created. If your natural inclination is to avoid geometric surfaces in favour of something more organic, please stay a while in this chapter and you will soon be a convert to pleats.

9.1_1
Not all pleated surfaces need to be measured and precise. Here, the run of mountain and valley folds is improvised, creating a pleasing interplay between exactness and spontaneity.

9.1_2 (opposite above left)
The traditional herringbone zigzag-pleat pattern always looks dynamic when lit from any angle. As the light moves, the pattern changes.

9.1_3 (opposite above right)
An unusual idea for a pleat pattern. The individual pieces are folded flat, then arranged in an overlapping pattern, much like tiles on a roof.

9.1_4 (opposite below left)
A long run of accordion pleats can be bent into a circular fan shape that always has great decorative appeal.

9.1_5 (opposite below right)
These fish scales are made by placing a pair of mountain and valley folds extremely close together, repeating the pattern across the sheet, then repeating the pattern again, perpendicularly across.

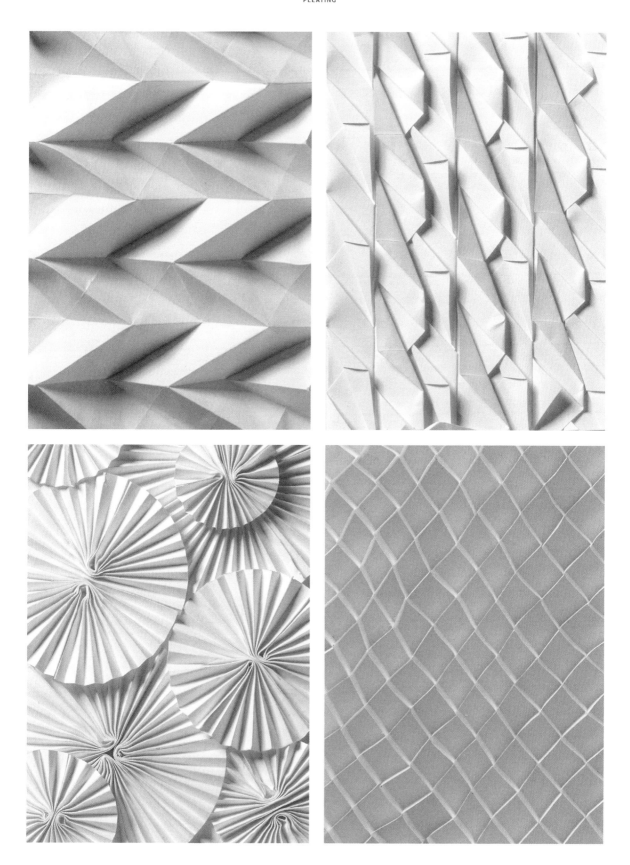

9.2
Two-colour Textures

The introduction of a second colour will allow you to create many new tones, particularly if the pleats are deep or bunched closely together. The temptation is to make the surface too rich and gratuitously decorative, so some restraint with colour is advised. Let the light and shade do the work, not the colour.

9.2_2 (below right)
Triangular fans are bunched together in a continuous path that winds across the sheet. Note how shadows fall on the blue backing sheet, creating their own pleating effect of light and shade.

9.2_1 (below left)
A herringbone pattern made in white paper has had triangular holes cut into it, revealing a darker surface behind, thus exaggerating the shadow effect on the paper.

9.2_3 (opposite)
Another herringbone pattern. The second colour is achieved by using a nail file to scratch away the purple ink that coated the sheet, to reveal the white card beneath.

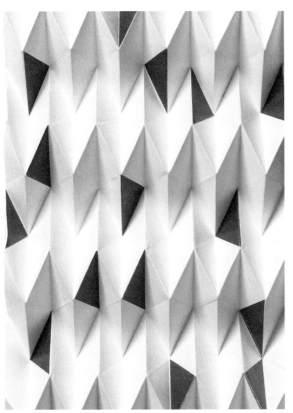

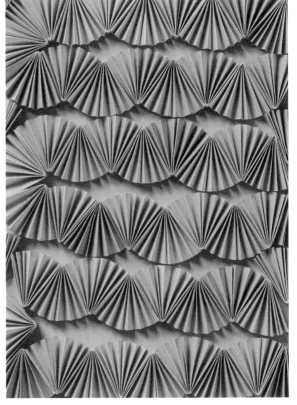

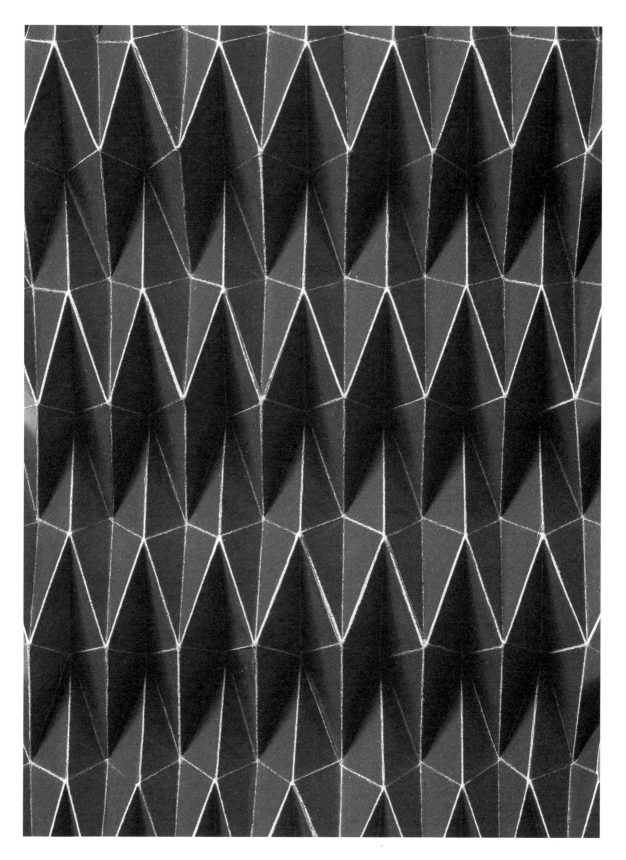

9.3
Multicolour Textures

Pleats are an excellent technique for adding detail to a texture. The many folds create complex patterns of light and shade, made more complex still as the number of colours increases. If you are intimidated by the technical sophistication of some of the designs in this chapter, simple pleats can look just as effective.

9.3_1
The fan motif seen before in the chapter is here rendered as a non-repeat surface. The piece was later scanned, converted into a repeat pattern and printed digitally on to fabric to create a stunning scarf.

9.3_2
In this highly creative work, strips of simple accordion pleats are turned sideways, so, from directly above, only the edges can be seen. As our viewpoint moves left or right, more coloured surfaces can be seen.

9.3_3
Basic V folds in several colours are laid against a coloured background, so that the many brightly lit and shaded facets flicker across the sheet to create a high-energy texture.

9.4
Taking it Further

There are an immense number of manufactured designs that can be considered pleated, in every conceivable material and at all scales. Indeed, the simple zigzag fold, whether three-dimensional or laid flat, can be considered the most ubiquitous of all texturing techniques. Here are a few examples to show the diversity of its use.

9.4_1
The fan motif on page 94 was photographed, manipulated into a repeat pattern, then digitally printed on to polyester to create a scarf that looks as though it might almost feel warm to the touch. Romi Messer, Shenkar College (Israel).

9.4_2
Two accurately made pleats gather the fabric
together, giving structure to the garment and
allowing it to drape elegantly over the
shoulder. Note how the pleats disappear
at the bust. Irina Dzhus (Ukraine).

9.4_3 (below and below right)
Tightly packed V-shaped pleats made from
folded alumimium create a linear curtain wall
from a distance but, closer to, appear more
swollen and organic. The vertical alignment
of the pleats minimizes the role of light and
shade. Vaillo + Irigaray (Spain).

10

Cut Pleats

This technique needs explaining step by step. When mastered, it will be possible to make any pop-up on any fold, to create very complex cut-and-fold surfaces.

Step 1
Create a simple zigzag pleat. Here, the paper is shown divided into four parts with a central 'valley' fold flanked by two 'mountain' folds, but it can be divided many more times. We will cut the centre fold, so unfold the folds to each side, retaining just the fold to be cut.

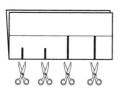

Step 2
With scissors, make four cuts. The two cuts on the left go halfway up to the crease line and the two on the right go exactly up to the crease line.

Step 3
Make two short horizontal folds that connect the two pairs of cuts.

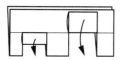

Step 4
Unfold the small folds, just made. It will make the next steps easier if you also fold them to the back, to make the folds very flexible.

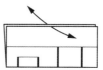

Step 5
Unfold the centre fold to create a shallow V.

Step 6
Push gently from below to 'pop' the two cut rectangles upwards. The top rectangle is bigger than the bottom one. Nothing will 'pop' if the paper is almost flat, or almost folded in half.

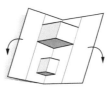

Step 7
Fold the left and right edges of the paper downwards, returning the paper to the 'M' shape seen in Step 1.

Step 8
This is the result, showing two types of pop-up of different sizes. With a longer zigzag of pleats, many more rows of pop-ups can be made. The pop-ups were made on the central valley fold, but the technique can be used on any fold, whether valley or mountain. Experiment with the shape of the cut, its angle, height or length and how 'pops' on neighbouring valley and mountain folds can touch or overlap.

10.1
White
Textures

Cut pleats are perhaps the most technically complex texturing technique in the book and take the most preparation. Nevertheless, even 15 minutes of practice will give you enough know-how to create surprisingly intricate textures. From there, the technique has no limits. Made in white paper, your work will always look stunning.

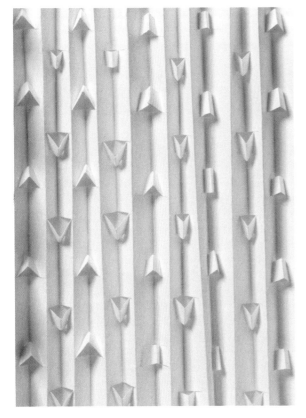

10.1_1 (left)
A simple zigzag accordion pleat is cut into with a series of small triangles, arranged in diagonal lines across the sheet, adding much visual interest to an otherwise basic folded texture.

10.1_2 (above)
This piece is technically similar to 10.1_1, but seen from the reverse side of the sheet. Here, the pleats are folded tightly together and the cut triangles invert downwards into the paper, instead of standing up.

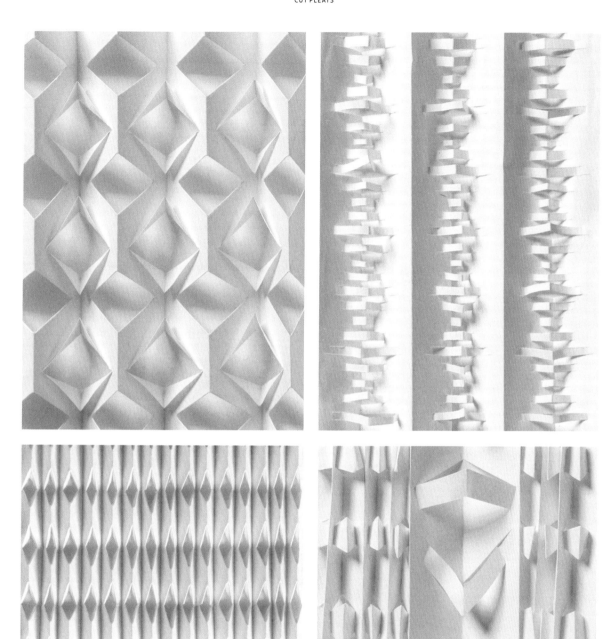

10.1_3 (top left)
A technically sophisticated texture made by
cutting and folding triangles on *every* fold
across the pleat, both valleys and mountains.
The precision of the folding and cutting adds
to its appeal.

10.1_4 (above left)
This piece is very similar to 10.1_2, opposite.
The main difference is that the tightly bunched
pleats have been pulled open so that the holes
created by the cutting are more visible.

10.1_5 (top right)
Many small rectangles are cut and 'popped'
upwards. Notice how the same size of
rectangle is seen when you look across the
sheet. This is because, when the paper was
folded, the pleats were compressed and
scissors cut through every layer at once.

10.1_6 (above right)
Large, simple cut pleats made on a single large
pleat are flanked by smaller cut pleats made
on much narrower pleats. The contrast of scale
creates much visual variety on what would
otherwise have been a simple repeat texture.

10.2
Two-colour Textures

The 'peekaboo' aesthetic of cut pleats allows colours to peep through the cuts, thus adding depth and interest to the single-sheet surface. When colours combine with the different tones of the folded and cut facets, which are either in the light or in the shade, the effect is a pleasingly complex texture.

10.2_1
A sequence of overlapping cut pleats creates a complex surface, enhanced by the darker colour beneath, which flashes into and out of view as our viewpoint changes.

10.2_2 (above left)
The cut pleats are made from a back layer
of paper that is folded identically to the top
layer. Rectangular holes cut in the top layer
are pierced by the pop-ups coming from the
layer beneath.

10.2_3 (above right)
Are the cut pleats popping upwards towards
the camera, or popping down, away from it?
It's difficult to know from the image. The
ambiguity has the effect of flattening
the surface.

10.2_4
An unusual pattern of folded pleats becomes
the basis for a series of cut pleats that pop
downwards to reveal a colour beneath.
Experiments with the folded surface will
always create interesting cut-pleat textures.

10.3
Multicolour Textures

Multicoloured cut-pleat surfaces offer us an opportunity to create highly complex textures, in which one dominant colour is complemented by speckles of others. More than most other techniques in this book, this one allows for an exuberant use of colour, turning the essentially geometric aesthetic into surfaces that are witty and playful.

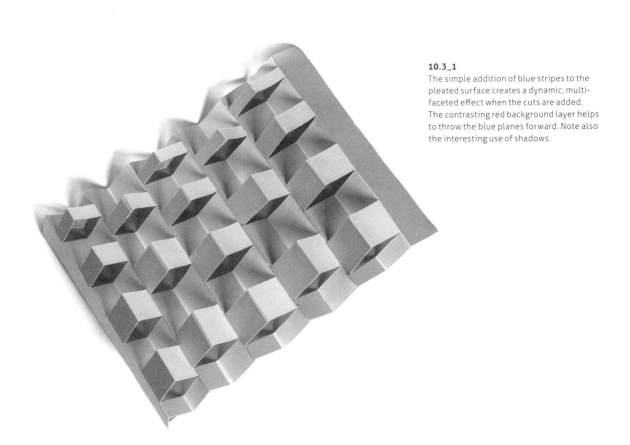

10.3_1
The simple addition of blue stripes to the pleated surface creates a dynamic, multi-faceted effect when the cuts are added. The contrasting red background layer helps to throw the blue planes forward. Note also the interesting use of shadows.

10.3_2
Similar to 10.3_1 opposite, but this time neutral grey is complemented by contrasting blue and orange papers, visible through the cuts. As always, movement around the piece will open and close the holes to reveal and hide the colours.

10.3_3 (below left)
Triangular cut pleats on both the mountain and valley folds of the folded pleats permit light and dark colours to be seen behind. Look closely and you will see that the folded pleat is not a simple accordion, but is interrupted by extra small pleats.

10.3_4 (below right)
Black is rarely a good colour with which to make textures, because it minimizes the shadows. White, being the palest, is usually best. Here, however, black is used to great effect, throwing forwards and giving attention to the many brightly coloured cut-pleat blocks.

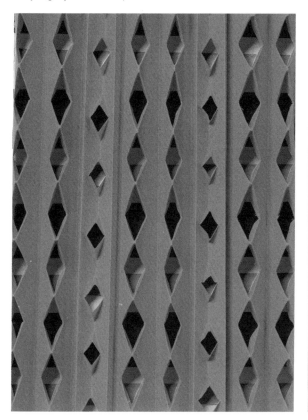

10.4
Taking it Further

The natural home of the cut pleat is in non-woven fabric, such as felt or bonded material, where the cuts can interact with the folded pleats without the material fraying. This creates very elaborate repeat textures that mix the formality of a necessarily geometric structure with the informality of soft fabric on the body.

10.4_1
Small cuts are used to open out, and open out again, a succession of ever-narrowing pleats to create sleeves in an otherwise simple cape form that drapes around the body, considerably increasing the apparent volume of the design. Alexandra Verschueren (Belgium).

10.4_2

By the same designer, these three images (and the one on the facing page) show the versatility of the cut-pleat technique in different fabrics, at different scales and for different garments. The best way to evolve a cut-pleat pattern is first to pleat a sheet of paper – A4 copy paper is ideal – and then to freely cut it, to see what patterns emerge. This period of experimentation will eventually lead to work that is more precisely made, but precision is not the place to start. Alexandra Verschueren (Belgium).

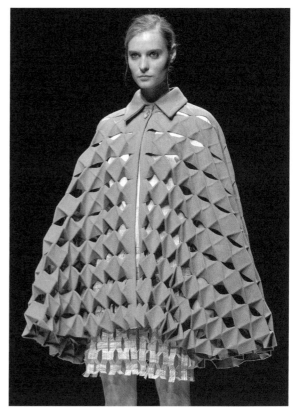

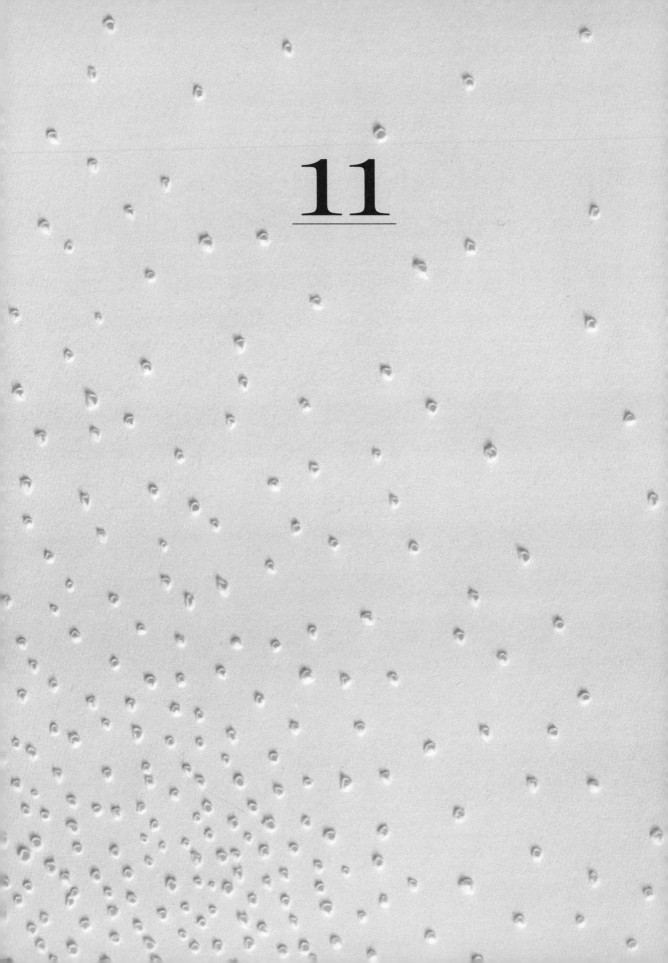

11

Stippling

Stippling, usually done with the point of a pen or pencil, is a technique in which a myriad of individual dots combine to create subtle shadow gradations. If the dots are of different colours, the technique is known as Pointillism, popularized by the French artist Georges Seurat (1859–91).

The stippling effect can also be achieved using the point of a needle, pushed through the surface of the paper. Clearly, the width of the shaft behind the sharp point will dictate the diameter of the hole. Try using needle points from as small as a sewing needle to as wide as a knitting needle.

One helpful tip is to create a soft surface under the paper (a sheet of foam or a folded towel), into which the needle point can bury itself after it has passed through the paper. If the surface under the paper is hard, only the very tip of the needle will pierce the paper and the hole will be very tiny.

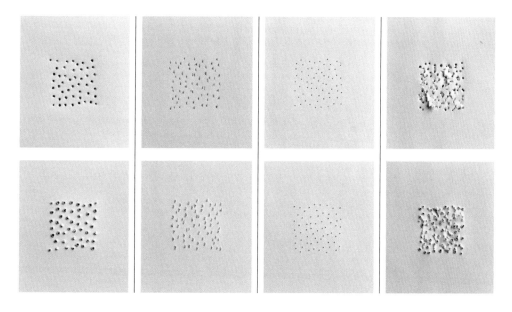

The top row shows the upper surface of sheets of paper that have had sharp points of different widths pushed through. The bottom row shows the underside. Note how the upper surfaces are clean but the undersides are much rougher.

11.1
White Textures

There is no escaping that stippling is a delicate effect, sometimes difficult to see from a distance. Nevertheless, close to, stippling is revealed as a very expressive texturing technique, able to create surfaces of great subtlety and accuracy. Many people find it to be a relaxing and meditative activity.

11.1_1
The surface is randomly stippled but given interest by the use of different stippling tools, which sometimes pierce the paper from the front and sometimes from the reverse.

11.1_2
Delicately stippled lines made with points of two different widths create a foliagelike texture. Although minimally worked, the surface appears complete and no further texturing is needed.

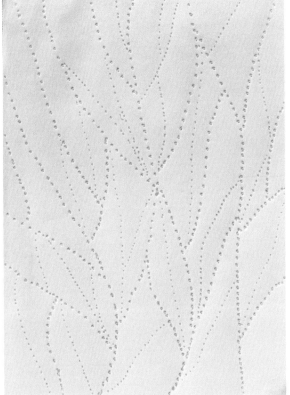

11.1_3

Intensely stippled rhombuses made with a very fine point to create an oblique chequerboard effect. Note the extreme precision with which the edge of each rhombus is rendered.

11.1_4

Triangles and swirls are stippled with points of different widths, leaving just enough of the surface unstippled to create a visible contrast between the two textures.

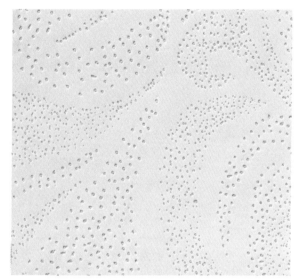

11.1_5

Holes made with a wide, blunt tip contrast with small circles of densely packed, narrow-tipped holes to create a delicate interplay between the two elements and the unstippled surface.

11.1_6

This simple but precisely executed stippled texture is here seen from the reverse side, so that flaps of paper are still covering most of the holes, allowing minute flecks of paper to be highlighted.

11.2
Two-colour Textures

Stippling creates only very small holes, so looking through them to see a second colour is all but impossible. The solution is simply to cut larger holes into the top layer through which the second colour can be seen, then to relate the areas of stippled texture to the cut-outs.

11.2_1 (below left)
At first sight, this is a series of parallelograms cut into the darker top surface, through which lighter blue is visible. Look again and a delicate stippling texture can also be seen.

11.2_2 (below right)
A combination of large cut-outs, revealing a putty-coloured backing sheet, and dense areas of stippled holes that echo the cut-outs, makes for a surface of textural contrasts.

11.2_3 (opposite)
Two sheets of card are placed together and geometric shapes cut from the grey top layer to reveal the beige card beneath. Then, different-sized stippling tools are pierced though both layers (it may be difficult to see the holes in the beige, under the grey layer).

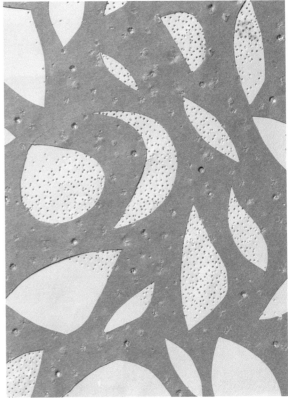

11.3
Multicolour
Textures

As the number of colours increases, the role of the stippled textures must, inevitably, diminish. If stippling is to be used effectively, however, a balance must be made between the two and one should never dominate the other. Always remember that you have great control over the stippled texture, by changing the width of the tip that pierces the paper and by choosing which side of the sheet is viewed.

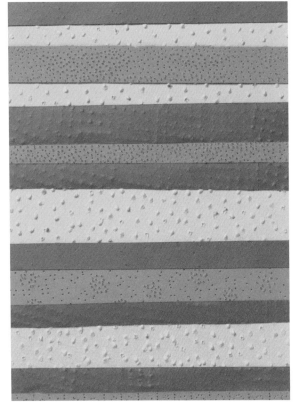

11.3_1
Strips of vibrant colours are stippled with tips of different widths, using different densities and different patterns, to create a surface texture that is understated but complex.

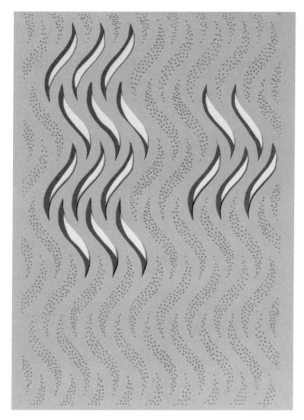

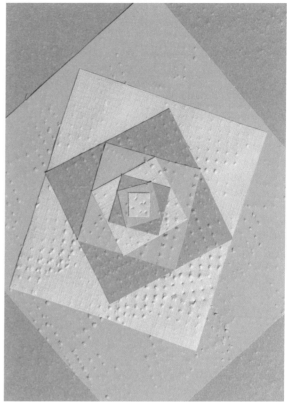

11.3_2 (above left)
Skilful stippling and the equally skilful cutting of the paper combine to make this unexpectedly fluid texture. Notice the absolute control over the stippling, ensuring that all the holes are equally spaced.

11.3_3 (above right)
Concentric squares were glued to create a flat surface, then the stippling technique was attempted through all the layers. Predictably, the thick layering would not be pierced, leading to the creation of dents, not holes.

11.3_4
Similar in technique to 11.2_3 on page 113, this piece combines thread with the paper, connecting up some of the stippled holes into a diagonal grid. Note the great control of the stippling and cutting, creating a complex series of surface patterns.

11.4
Taking it Further

This most inconsequential-sounding of texturing techniques is a hidden gem. Used discerningly, it can create intriguing surfaces in any material, both decorative and functional. If you are looking to give a conventional design an unconventional twist, try experimenting with different styles of stippling to activate the surface.

11.4_1
Made in perforated aluminium to achieve a delicate lacelike effect, the chair is finished with an epoxy-polyester paint so that it can be used outdoors. Note the simple fold across the front of the seat and how the perforations continue between the front legs. Ex'primae (France).

11.4_2
This Nike ProTurboSpeed suit features a grid of small doughnut-shaped stipples. In much the same way that dimples on a golf ball allow it to fly further, the stipples allow a runner to move faster through the air. Nike, Inc. (USA).

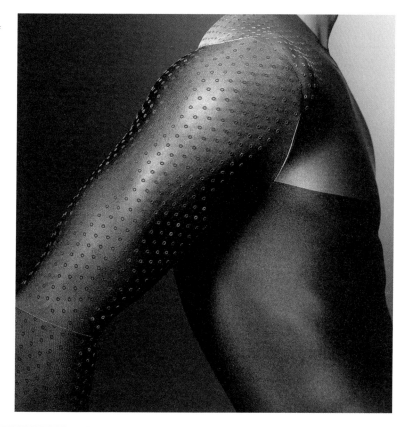

11.4_3
These slipcast bowls, made by allowing liquid clay to solidify in a mould, feature a roughly stippled surface that gives an unusual and highly tactile texture to a conventional form. Oscar Copping (UK).

12

Translucent Surfaces

Of the 12 textures presented in the book, this is the one with a difference. Whereas all the others are lit from the front, translucent surfaces are lit from the back. To achieve the effect, two things are needed: a strong light source, such as a light table, scanner (or photocopier) with an open lid, or an external window; and paper that is translucent, not opaque. The strength of the light source and the translucency of the paper need to be in balance, so that the effect is neither too dark nor too light.

Rectangular sheets of tissue paper are overlaid one on another, so that the surface progressively darkens as the layers accumulate. The effect is easy to achieve, but dramatic.

Orange tissue paper is collaged together, so that the tones range from a light orange to a very dark brown. Careful layering of the sheets can thus create almost any tone.

When different colours of tissue are used, the total number of colours and tones achieved becomes very large. They can be unexpectedly dark, pale or vibrant. At first, just experiment!

12.1
White
Textures

Many shades of grey, from almost pure white to almost black, can be achieved with just a simple sheet of white tissue paper. It's an exciting and instantly rewarding process: have an idea, layer the pieces and then light it from behind to see what you have made.

12.1_1
A sheet of tracing paper was crumpled into a ball, then opened flat. The distress caused to the sheet by this process means that parts of it become opaque. The same effect could be achieved with straight-line folds.

12.1_2
Circles of paper are carefully overlapped in a grid to create this simple pattern. It would be worthwhile to attempt the same pattern with different colours of tissue paper.

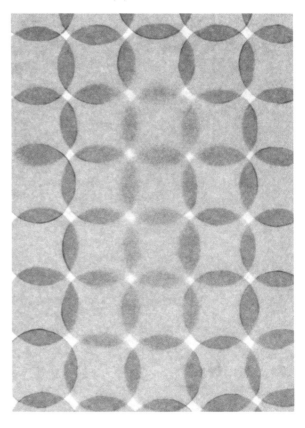

12.1_3 (above)
Three different approaches to creating translucent textures, made by holding and then twisting the centre of the paper, by creating a pleated fan, and by overlapping many squares of paper.

12.1_4 (right)
Multiple strips are laid crossways in this image to create a very delicate texture that could almost have been made with charcoal. The image appears a little out of focus because the layers are not pressed together, thus casting fuzzy shadows on to each other.

12.1_5 (below)
These two images show the opposite extremes of layering paper: one is improvised and spontaneous, the other highly structured and geometric. Which style is more appealing to you?

12.2
Two-colour Textures

Using two colours when creating translucent textures does not mean working with just a second colour, but working with a second set of tones – and even a third set, when the two tones are combined. This can create a dizzying set of colour and tonal possibilities that two opaque sheets of paper could never equal.

12.2_1
Printed cases for cupcakes were used to create this translucent surface, which begins as a regular pattern in the bottom left-hand corner, but is increasingly randomized by the time it has reached the opposite corner.

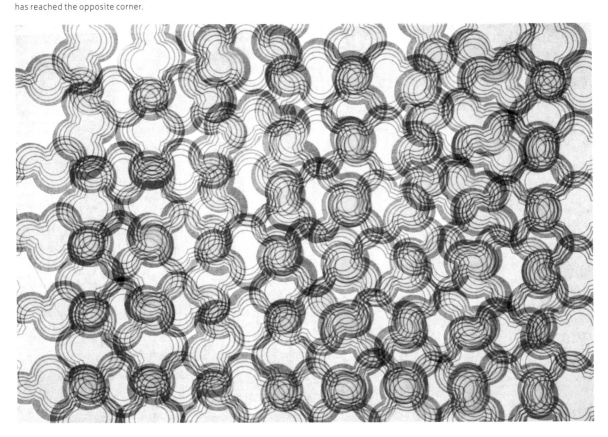

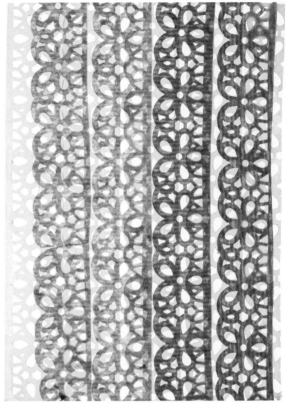

12.2_2 (above left)
Blue and white sheets of tissue were overlaid
to create this repeat pattern, and glued
together without reference to a previously
drawn grid so that it becomes informal rather
than rigidly geometric.

12.2_3 (above right)
Silver and gold cake-decorating ribbons were
placed side by side, and also arranged in
layers, to create this dramatic pattern. What
other found objects can you use?

12.3_4
Triangles of blue plastic gel were used here.
The thickness and relative opacity of the gel,
however, meant that after only three layers
the surface was almost black.

12.3
Multicolour Textures

Suddenly, a riot of colour! The large number of tones and shades achievable by overlapping different colours is given greater intensity by the use of light, so that textures of unusual vivacity are created. It is worth noting that the bright colours are not the product of coloured light, but are brightly lit, coloured pigments. The pigments will combine to create darker shades.

12.3_1
Handmade papers flecked with plant fibres were simply folded to create this richly textured, organic-looking surface. Note the many subtly different tones and strands of fibres that add interest to an otherwise simple texture.

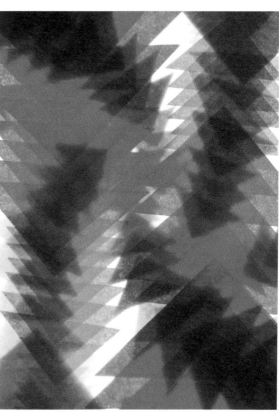

12.3_2 (above left)
A narrow palette of yellow, orange and red tissue-paper triangles are overlapped in two opposing lines that produce a great many vibrant tones. This is the first of three studies on this page which eventually led to the creation of the printed scarf on page 126.

12.3_3 (above right)
This time an expanded palette of colours and a dynamic spiralling of the triangles create more colour options, set starkly against a white background. Note the subtle mottled surfaces of the tissue paper.

12.3_4 (right)
Finally, a composition of triangles in which many lines of contrasting colours are overlaid to create a dense composition with darker tones than before.

12.4
Taking it Further

For designers, working with translucent surfaces presents many unique challenges, the greatest of which is to use well the effect that light has on a material when it passes *through*, rather than when it falls *on* it. Backlighting conjures a world of ethereal beauty and has often been used down the centuries to uplift the spirits.

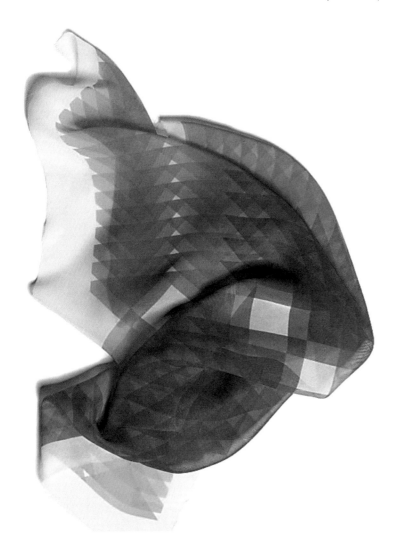

12.4_1
The samples on page 125 were reworked in Adobe Illustrator using percentage transparency fills of colour, then printed on to translucent polyester. When worn as a scarf, the gatherings of the material allow colours from underneath to be seen through the top layer, adding to the translucent effect. Although not itself backlit, the scarf used the qualities of backlighting as its inspiration. Iris Hagag, Shenkar College (Israel).

12.4_2 (above)
Made from hand-carved porcelain, these backlit tiles create an illuminated splashback for a kitchen work surface (note the size of the dish and book for a sense of scale). Amy Frankie Smith (UK) for Flux Surface.

12.4_3 (right)
Porcelain, fibreglass and glass combine to create scenic artworks evocative of Nordic light. The pieces have an appropriately epic scale, but are only 20cm (8in) high and 5cm (2in) deep. Helen Mørken (Norway).

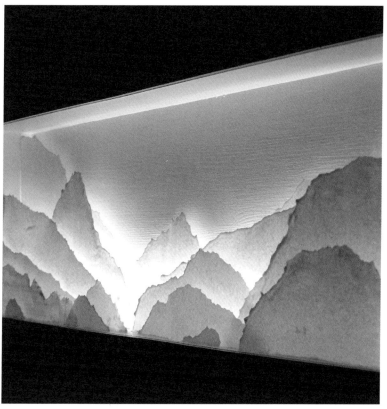

Acknowledgments

I would like to thank the second- and third-year BA Hons students in the Department of Textile Design at Shenkar College of Engineering, Design and Art in Tel Aviv, for creating the wonderful white and coloured samples seen in the book, and also for the almost 200 other wonderful samples that could not be used due to lack of space. The students are:

Gal Arev, Shani Avrahami, Tal Bar-El, Lurin Basha, Tal Betzalel, Maya Ferera, Iris Hagag, Tal Haiblum, Oleg Ioffe, Ira Klempner, Michal Luria, Leetal Marshall, Lyam Mayer, Yarden Menahem, Romi Messer, Diana Nurujnik, Sapir Oz, Tal Rosenthal, Hadar Rozenbaum, Noga Sapir, Orit Shahaf, Lital Shunak, Ella Siman-Tov, Avigail Weiss, Neta Ziv and Mor Zohar.

The cover shows a texture created by Tal Haiblum.

My thanks to Dr Katya Oicherman, Head of Textile Design at Shenkar College, for permission to work with her students.

Thanks also to the numerous students encountered over 30 years on many different art and design courses in several countries who road-tested paper textures. The idea for the book – and its structure – came from what you made.

Finally, my thanks to the many artists and designers who generously gave permission for their work to be included in the book.

Picture credits

All the line illustrations and samples on the first page of each chapter were created by the author. All the White, Two-colour and Multicolour Textures in the book were created by the students listed in the Acknowledgments. The students are identified by their initials. Where there is more than one image on a page, the credits are given left to right for the top row, then the middle row, then the bottom row.

p.4 TH **p.8** RM **p.10** TH ML **p.11** TB-E TR SA **p.12–13** & **p.14–15** co-made by SA & LS **p.18** AW **p.20** MF GA **p.21** LeM RM LB AW **p.22** LS **p.23** ML ML LS **p.24** LS LS **p.25** ML ML **p.28** IH **p.30** TB-E MF **p.31** AW YM NS **p.32** SO SO **p.33** NZ **p.34** SO **p.35** NZ NZ SO **p.38** ES **p.40** MZ **p.41** MF ES-T YM **p.42** IK **p.43** DN IK DN **p.44** DN IK **p.45** DN **p.48** Paul Jackson **p.50** GA **p.51** SO YM AW **p.52** TB **p.53** TB MZ **p.54** MZ **p.55** TB MZ **p.58** TR **p.60** SO **p.61** TH DN LeM ES **p.62** OS GA **p.63** OS GA **p.64** OS **p.65** GA GA **p.68** MF **p.70** IH TR **p.71** IK LeM RM **p.72** TH TB **p.73** TH **p.74** YM **p.75** YM YM TH **p.78** TR **p.80** YM NS **p.81** MZ MF IH TR **p.82** LB **p.83** LB MF MF **p.84** LB LB **p.85** MF MF **p.88** TR **p.90** TH **p.91** NS LM IK MF **p.92** TR RM **p.93** RM **p.94** RM **p.95** RM TR **p.98** MF **p.100** NZ YM **p.101** TR IH AW LM **p.102** NS **p.103** NS AW AW **p.104** NS **p.105** AW AW NS **p.108** NS **p.110l** NZ **p.111** AW RM OI OS **p.112** LY OI **p.113** LM **p.114** OI **p.115** LM OI LM **p.118** ES **p.120** TB NS **p.121** TR IH DN LM LS-T TH **p.122** ES **p.123** ES ES IH **p.124** E-ST **p.125** IH IH IH.

All photography by Meidad Suchovolski except for the images below.

p.16 © Valérie Buess. Part of Abot/Artists' Books on Tour, Vienna 2011 (Recognition Award); **p.17t** © Dana Bloom. Photo: Leonid Padrul, © Eretz Israel Museum, Tel Aviv; **p.17b** Torc: Dianne King, Photo: William Van Esland; **p.26** Artist: Larry Schulte, Collection: Museum of Nebraska Art, Kearney, NE; **p.27t** Design by Kensuke Aisaka. Photo © Shigeo Ogawa; **p.27b** © Grant Rooney / Alamy Stock Photo; **p.36** Layers Cloud Chair by Richard Hutten for Kvadrat. Photo © Casper Sejersen; **p.37t** © Lucente Brand of Gruppo Rostirolla SRL. Brian Rasmussen (Designer). Photo: Daniele Di Pietro; **p.37b (all)** © Vadim Kibardin; **p.46l&r** © Anna Stepankova, Tamashii Chair was a Bachelor work in 2012, Tomas Bata University, Zlin. Photography by Vendula Knopová; **p.47l&r** © Moshe Gordon. Photo: Leonid Padrul, © Eretz Israel Museum, Tel Aviv; **p.56l&r** © Ida Rak. Photo: Leonid Padrul, © Eretz Israel Museum, Tel Aviv; **p.57** The Midnight Dress by Felicity Brown (www.FelicityBrown.com)/ Photo: Thomas Cooksey; **p.66** © Made in Ratio. Designer: Brodie Neill; **p.67t** Design Tom Raffield. Courtesy John Lewis. www.johnlewis.com, 03456 049049; **p.67b** © Hadar Rozenbaum. Photo © Paul Jackson; **p.76l&r** Courtesy John Lewis. www.johnlewis.com, 03456 049049; **p.77t** © Geoffrey Nees. Handcut and folded paper relief 2005; **p.77b** © VIEW Pictures Ltd / Alamy Stock Photo; **p.86 all** © kna plus corporation; **p.87t** © Blå Station AB, Design: 04i 2013, Photo: Erik Karlsson; **p.87cl&cr** © Meirav Barzilay; **p.87bl&br** © Elisa Strozyk. Photos by "STUDIO BEEN"; **p.96** © Romi Messer. Photo © Meidad Suchovolski; **p.97t** © Irina Dzhus. Collection: Totalitarium, Season: Autumn/Winter 2015. Photographer: Olga Nepravda. Stylist: MUA & Hair Stylist: Irina Dzhus. Model Viera Stankeieva; **p.97bl & br** © José Manuel Cutillas Medina / www.josemacutillas.com; **p.106–7 all** © Didier Messens/Getty Images; **p.116** © Exprimae/Metal Design Concept. Design: Buck Design; **p.117t** © Nike; **p.117b** © Oscar Copping; **p.126** © Iris Hagag. Photo © Meidad Suchovolski; **p.127t** Photo: Ross Phillips, Forest Eyes Photography, www.foresteyes.co.uk; Artist: Amy Frankie Smith, Flux Surface, Translucent Porcelain Surfaces, www.fluxsurface.com; **p.127b** © Helen Mørken.